SYMMETRICAL WARM-UPS

Short Daily Exercises to Build Flexibility and Strength

by Christos Tsitsaros

CONTENTS

ISBN: 978-1-4234-7541-5

In Australia Contact:
Hal Leonard Australia Pty. Ltd.
4 Lentara Court
Cheltenham, Victoria, 3192 Australia
Email: ausadmin@halleonard.com.au

Visit Hal Leonard Online at
www.halleonard.com

Preface

The benefits of warming up sufficiently before practicing have been the subject of various studies in keyboard journals and scientific publications on performance health and medicine. One of the key issues discussed by researchers is the nature of the warm-up session. While a great deal of recent research has opened up new perspectives on alternative techniques for the purpose of conditioning the muscles and ligaments before activity (those include stretching, yoga poses, and mental preparation), one of the easiest and safest ways to warm up remains to simply perform the activity for a short time period at a lower rate and intensity. Christine Zaza in an article in *Medical Problems for Performing Artists* states: "A musical (i.e., neuromuscular) warm-up may be sufficient to protect against injury..." She also points out that stretching may entail considerable dangers because musicians have the tendency to perform stretches "overzealously" or incorrectly, as they often learn such methods from their peers instead of trained professionals. She therefore recommends the musical warm-up since "it is unlikely to cause any harm to musicians, because it consists of their usual musical activity performed at a reduced level."

The purpose of this collection is to help young pianists and more seasoned players condition their physical apparatus (fingers, hands, arms, shoulders, back), and prepare them for the ensuing task in a progressive, non-invasive way that does not over-exert the muscles through excessive repetition. A warm-up session needs to be safe if it is to serve as preparatory stage for the activity to follow, and as a means to optimize performance and protect against injury.

To this end, the warm-ups in this volume are:

In progressive difficulty. Usually, a simple preparatory warm-up leads to a more complex one. This is particularly helpful to younger players, who may need to stay longer with easier patterns, before moving to more demanding ones.

Relatively short. Many of them consist of just a few measures. Others are chained in longer segments and combine repetitions of a motive in different positions and variations.

Symmetrical. The very mirror-like nature of our hands provided the inspiration for this permeating feature. Contrary motion promotes likewise movements in both hands, which results in one hand teaching the other. In time the student will realize that it is easier to perform similar motions with both arms than different ones simultaneously.

Based on the physiology of the hand and its proper relation to the keys. The shape of each motive is designed to help the student form a natural, healthy, and strong hand shape combined with a proper hand/forearm alignment.

Beyond lending themselves as warm-ups, these short exercises also aim to increase proper hand shape awareness, improve arm/hand alignment, and cultivate the indispensable arm motions that facilitate and empower the fingers, as well as ward off fatigue. The role of flexibility and connection becomes immediately apparent, forming the key to a unified thought system that literally regards fingers as the far extremities of the arm, never separating them from their original source. In this sense, finger strength hinges on the proper use of the arm, both with regards to hand form and alignment, as well as motion. Following these concepts, the student will eventually achieve a stronger sense of connection within the entire body.

The point of support and the hand form: ideas from Chopin's *Sketches for a Piano Method.*

Chopin makes an insightful analogy of the fingers being in relation to the arm the equivalent of what the feet are to the body: supports of its natural weight. In his unfinished *Sketches for a Piano Method*, he states: "The arm from its attachment to the shoulder must assume a perfect suppleness and the fingers find the point of support on the keyboard, which supports everything. The beauty of the sound and its volume depend on the weight that results from the heaviness of the arm and hand combined."

Based on this idea, Chopin goes as far as dismissing any school that places "an exaggerated emphasis on the thumb by placing it further in the keys instead of touching the outside edge of the key on its tip." Further on, he elaborates: "Due to its formation, the thumb does not properly speaking belong in the hand; the hand consists of the four fingers and the role of the thumb is to serve as its counterpart and auxiliary. In this way, it plays the important role of renewing the hand, and making a new beginning when the four fingers have played through. It must stay the least possible on the keys, near the end of the keys, ready to assume its renewing role."

A direct application of his technique can be seen in his next statement: "This thumb position is what facilitates scales and arpeggios. An inclined thumb pressed in hinders the movement of the fingers, whereas one that is placed on the edge, finds itself at the convenient spot to either pass under the fingers in the ascending mode or allow the other fingers to pass over it, in the descending."

Chopin provides yet another valuable explanation for adopting this particular position, namely the simple physical rule upon which all levers function with more power when they are in straight line. Therefore, in placing the hand, he tries to maintain the straightness of the levers, from the elbow to the tip of the fingers. To this effect he prescribes: "Touch the 5th finger always immediately below the black key and the thumb on the edge of the white key."

The warm-ups in this volume are based precisely on the idea of the thumb forming the counterpart of the four fingers. Therefore, in teaching or practicing them, it is crucial that the hand is placed in straight alignment with the arm, and that the thumb is neither bent nor placed too far in the keys; furthermore, the longer fingers should be naturally curved in and the fifth finger should face down toward the keys.

Hand movement

Chopin cautions against stiffness and prescribes certain "graceful" and helpful movements, within limits. Clearly against too much movement, in scales and arpeggios he advises letting the thumb come off the key once the second finger presses the next note, and joining it (the second finger) with a supple and quick movement. In applying this in a five-finger passage, one perceives a slight, lateral movement of the hand toward the fifth finger in ascending passages, and from the fifth to the thumb in descending ones. This natural motion conforms to the idea of assigning the four fingers (2-5) their function as supporting props for the arm, finding the point of support on the key bed. In describing this movement in scales, the great Russian pedagogue Heinrich Neuhaus in his *Art of Piano Playing* states that "the forearm is in constant and smooth motion, the wrist turns when and as needed, and thanks to this the fingers strike the keys and are always, at every instant, in the most favorable and convenient position for so doing."

This dynamic forearm/finger relation precludes any static hand position. The use of the right movements results in a feeling of ease, readiness at all times, and connection of fingers and arm. The degree of the movement naturally depends on the tempo, the type of figuration, as well as the type of sound the music requires.

Fingering

Carl Philipp Emanuel Bach in his famous *Essay on the True Art of Playing Keyboard Instruments* talks about a new way of fingering suitable for the more melodic passages in use during his time, in contrast to the predominantly polyphonic style of earlier periods. He informs us that, before his father's time, keyboardists avoided the use of the thumb. The frequent use of all the tonalities, along with significant changes in musical taste, led his father to devise a new way of fingering that broadly enlarged the use of the thumb, elevating its role to the principal finger and the key to all fingering. In his chapter on fingering, he talks extensively about the "change of fingers," a term he uses to describe the passing of the thumb underneath the fingers and the crossing of the fingers over the thumb.

Chopin continues some of Bach's fingering ideas, but takes them a step further, emancipating the thumb even more and using it on black keys quite more frequently than Bach, who suggests the application of that technique only in arpeggiated chord passages and large intervals. Chopin also experimented with crossing the thumb under the little finger and *vice versa*.

The singing legato was Chopin's main concern in his use of fingering. In search of that, he unashamedly revisited older masters, such as François Couperin, who also emphasized connection through fingering. His infusion of the traditional fingering system with more crossings (long over short), silent substitutions, or unorthodox fingerings reflect his adherence to the bel canto style of playing and effort to ensure a perfect legato.

The exercises in this volume are mainly based on the traditional fingering system outlined by C. P. E. Bach. In certain instances however, alternative fingerings are provided. Those include crossings of long fingers over short (ex. section B: 6a, m. 217), and the use of the thumb on black keys in five-finger sequences and scalar patterns (ex. section A: 13d, m. 93).

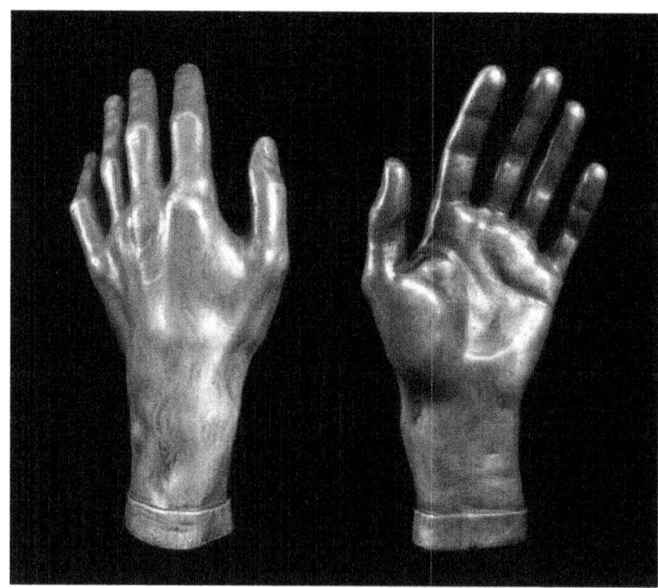

Cast of Chopin's left hand (bronze) by Auguste Clésinger

Introduction

Preparation for the warm-up session

Prior to warming up, it is important that the student is seated correctly: halfway back on the bench, both feet squarely touching the floor, at a height that places the elbows at a slight inclination over the white key level, and at a distance that allows reaching the two ends of the keyboard without bending sideways on either side. In trying to attain good posture, the pianist must keep the torso open and elongated, with the middle of the back toned, and the shoulders soft and relaxed. In order to move freely for register shifts, it is important to be sure that the pelvis is never blocked and that the entire back is aligned: the neck with the spine and the ribcage sitting on top of the hips. This centered and aligned posture ensures freedom and control, as well as balance and mobility. Moving flexibly in and out of the optimal position is perfectly natural and admissible, as long as the main core alignment is there to support all levers. A strong core grounded on a flexible foundation, with the two points of support the floor and the key bed, is the ideal one must try to achieve. Often, an overly loose upper back strives to compensate for rigidity and lack of mobility in the pelvic region. Slouching or contorting of the upper body, tensing of the neck and facial muscles, and stiffening of the forearms and fingers are all symptoms of a postural imbalance. Recognizing the signs of a disconnected physical approach forms the key to re-educating the student and the prerequisite for the proper utilization of the warm-ups. As with hand form, one comes to understand that good posture never implies rigidity or stiffness. In fact, movement initiated in the right places is not a mere aesthetic element but an integral ingredient in the acquisition of ease and optimal use of the body.

How to use the warm-ups

The warm-ups are divided into three sections:

A. **Adjacent notes and intervals** (from the second to the tenth and various combinations).

B. **Scales** (preparatory exercises, uninterrupted major and minor scale sequences, chromatic scalar patterns).

C. **Arpeggiated figures and chord preparation.**

Unless specified, all exercises are to be transposed into various keys, each key offering opportunities for meaningful fingering adjustments. Certain warm-ups are given in keys other than C major, for the purpose of exemplifying fingerings for keys that contain sharps or flats. In transposing, it will be necessary to constantly adjust the fingering in order to accommodate new positions. Experimentation with a number of fingering possibilities is strongly encouraged. One of the goals of this series is to make the student aware of various fingering patterns and solutions. Chromatic scale exercises and warm-ups that move chromatically can be launched on any key or register (ex. Section B:10a-11d).

Following are terms that are used in the warm-ups:

Et seq. When the term Et seq. (*et sequens*, "and so forth") is used, the warm-up is to be continued in the same manner, transferring the pattern diatonically up or down within a key (ex. section A:21b), or chromatically if the exercise is so designed (ex. section A:18g).

Et seq. al. When *et sequens al* ("and so forth up to") is used, the ending of the exercise, in either the ascending or descending mode, is provided after the light double bar (ex. section A:18b).

Light double bars are also provided in sequences of similar exercises, each one presenting a different variation. In such cases, the pianist is encouraged to alter the variation with each subsequent transposition or continue with a single pattern that feels right (ex. section C: 24e-24l).

Select your own items from the warm-up menu and design your own session according to your needs, readiness, time availability, and even the type of piece you are about to practice. The order is not important; at any time you can skip to a different warm-up in any key. Similarly, you do not have to go through all twelve keys at all times; transposing the warm-up in one or two selected keys works just as well. Use your creativity to vary the warm-ups, following the different versions provided in the book or creating your own by modifying the existing ones. You can do this in a number of ways: by changing the intervals or order of notes, transferring the pattern in different octaves, adding notes to chords, using minor instead of major, inverting the direction and motion, or using a different starting point in the left hand (i.e. playing the warm-up in parallel tenths or sixths.) You will equally benefit from combining two or more warm-ups into a larger synthesized exercise (ex. section A, 14b and c).

Three sample warm-up sessions:

Warm-up A.

Section A: 4b/5a (interchangeably), 6a (partial), 12, 11a-e (alternating variations with each transposition), 13a, 21b and c, 30a, 32b.

Section B: 4a and b (alternating variations), 7a and/or 8a (partial).

Section C: 5c, 21a-e (varying the pattern in each transposition), 31.

Warm-up B.

Section A: 1a and b, 8b, 10c, 13b, 17b and c, 21d, 23a (depending on the hand stretch and level of student), 30b.
Section B: 5a or b (partial).
Section C: 1a and b, 10, 21f, 23a-d.

Warm-up C.

Section A: 4a-d (alternating variations), 8a (partial), 14a and b, 15c, 18c and d, 22b, 29a and b, 31, 34c.
Section B: 6a, 10a-e (connected).
Section C: 23e-i (alternating patterns in each transposition), 25a, 26g and h.

Experiment practicing the warm-ups in the following ways:

- In a mildly slow tempo, *piano* to *mezzo-piano*, with clear and slightly exaggerated hand motion. This is the ideal way to start a session as it gently sets the forearm motions underway and progressively conditions the muscles.
- Softly but firmly, in a light staccato, emphasizing strong fingertip activity.
- *Mezzo-forte, legato*, at a moderate tempo, somewhat reducing the hand travel.
- *Forte staccato, moderato*, with energetic fingertip action and even less hand travel.
- Fast, *leggiero, piano*, with smooth, discreet hand travel and very active fingertips, in close proximity to the keys.
- Fast, *forte*, with very active fingertips and responsive forearm motions to the extent they are needed. Phrased in various ways, in a range of speeds and dynamic levels.

It is essential to avoid *tempi* that are too slow, as they tend to isolate the fingers from the rest of the arm. Always work your way through easier exercises in milder *tempi* to faster speeds and more demanding exercises. Try transposing in distant keys, including those containing several sharps or flats. Black keys provide excellent points of support; the less black keys in a passage, the more difficult it is to built the hand position that allows for the fluidity of the arm motion. Always work in a relaxed manner, using the arms flexibly and the body as economically and wisely as possible, avoiding periodic concomitant movements, such as counting with the head or leaning back and forth with every change of dynamic change. Finally, allow short breaks between exercises in order to give the muscles the opportunity to adjust and recuperate.

Very importantly, avoid playing the exercises out of their rhythmic context, which is likely to result in an isolated and disconnected physical approach. The main goal is to tie the exercises to the breath and appropriate motion. According to Chopin "the goal of the exercises is not to learn to perform a passage, but to form the hand, and to turn it into a fine instrument, capable of performing all similar difficulties ensuing from a model exercise."

Benefits of using the warm-ups

- Increased sense of hand/arm alignment and connection with the entire back and rest of the body.
- Development of a natural hand position based on rational ideas that allow for support of the arm on the key bed, the fingers acting as arm props.
- Cultivation of facilitating arm motions, and increased overall flexibility.
- Progressive expansion of finger stretch, not only the reach between thumb and fifth finger but also of the in-between stretches.
- Adequate and progressive preparation before working on repertoire as a way of warming-up for the task and warding off injury.
- Significant improvement of aural skills and development of the internal ear through transposition.
- Use of creativity in designing warm-up sequences and altering them according to individual needs.
- Increased awareness of good fingering habits that conform to the relation of the hand shape to the keyboard; with that, readiness and experience in fingering adjustment.
- Re-education of the poorly aligned or injured pianist. I attribute all injuries to a combination of poor postural alignment, lack of connection of hand, arm, and rest of the body, as well as a poor hand position that hinders arm flexibility and precludes the feeling of support on the keyboard.

It is my sincere wish that these exercises, the product of my own experience as pianist and teacher, will help students attain their full artistic potential by cultivating and refining their technical means in the long search of an ideal balance between mind and body.

—Christos Tsitsaros

References

Carl Philipp Emanuel Bach. *Essay on the True Art of Playing Keyboard Instruments*. New York: Norton & Company, Inc. 1949, edited and translated by William J. Mitchell.

Frédéric Chopin. *Esquisses Pour Une Méthode de Piano*. Texts gathered and presented by Jean-Jacques Eigeldinger. Flammarion, 1993.

François Couperin. *L'Art de Toucher le Clavecin*. Edited and translated by Margery Halford. Second edition, Alfred Publishing Co., Inc., 1995.

Jean-Jacques Eigeldinger. *Chopin Pianist and Teacher*. Cambridge University Press, Cambridge, 1986.

Heinrich Neuhaus. *The Art of Piano Playing*. Longwood Academic, Durango, Colorado, 1989.

Christine Zaza. *Research-Based Prevention for Musicians*. Medical Problems of Performing Artists, March 1994, pp. 3-6.

Symmetrical Warm-ups

Section A–Adjacent notes and intervals

Three natural positions. Observe the hand form, keeping the thumb perpendicular at the edge of the white key.

Transpose all following warm-ups chromatically in all 12 or select keys.

(Also, practice the same pattern in minor)

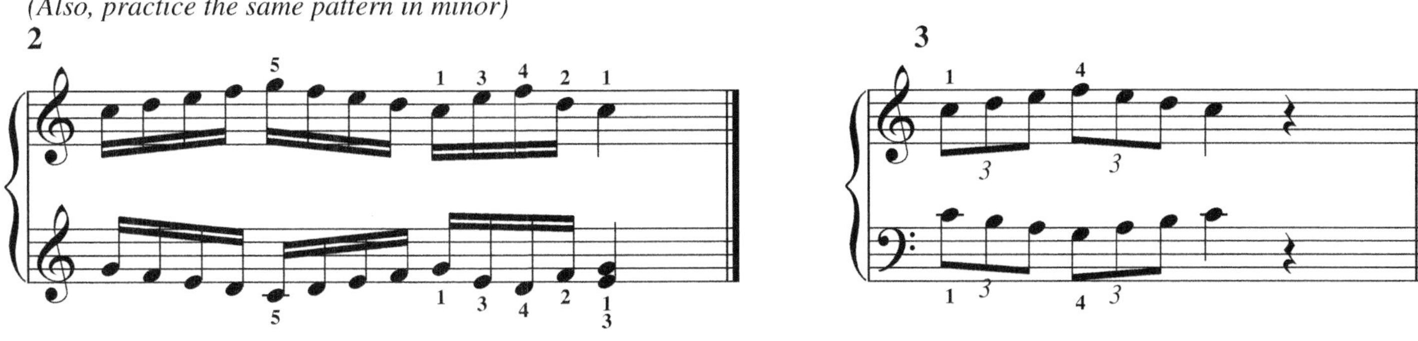

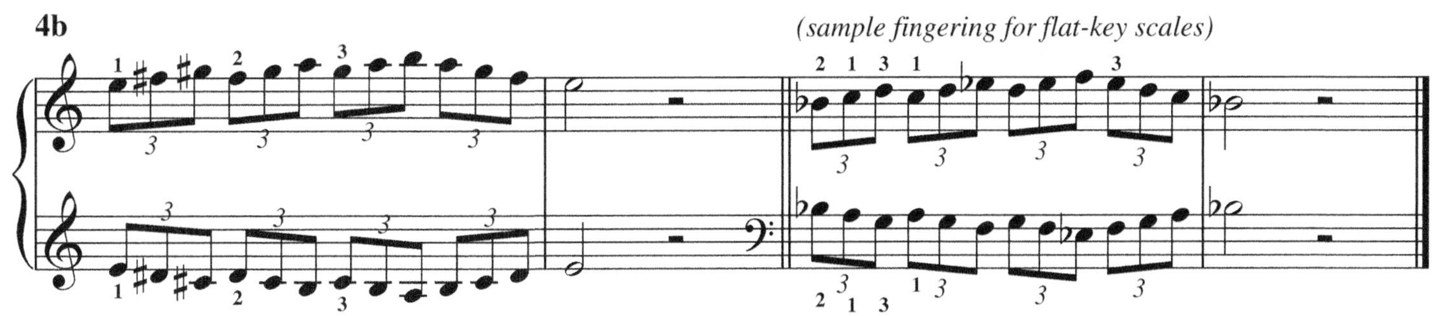

4c

4d

5a

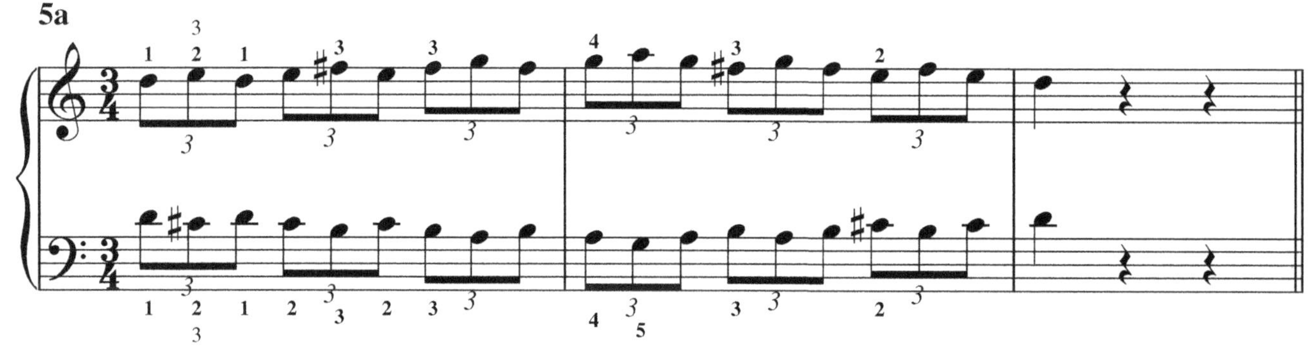

(sample fingering for flat-key scale)

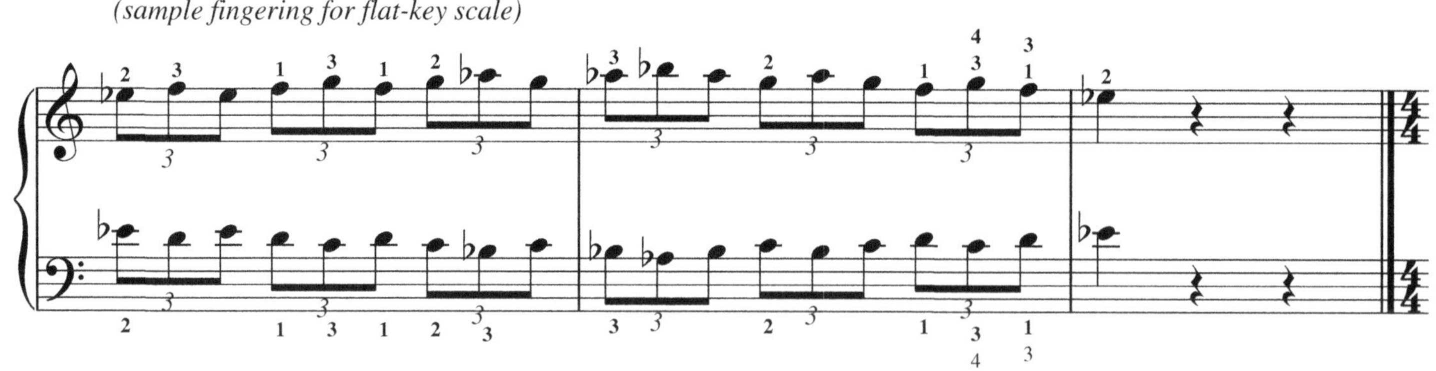

5b

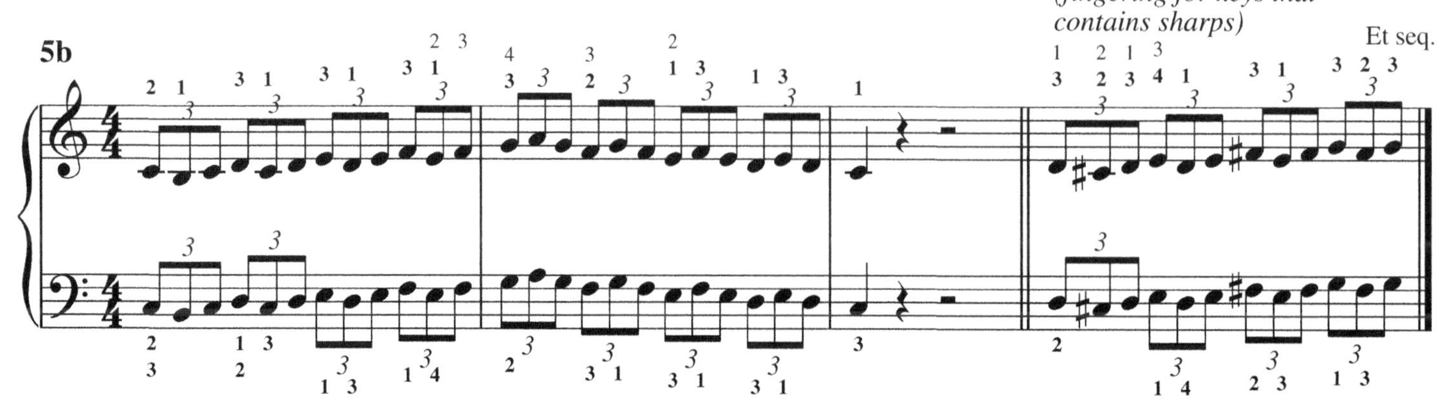

Perform the following warm-up very *legato* throughout, especially between measures.
(This exercise is given in all its transpositions so it can begin on any key.)

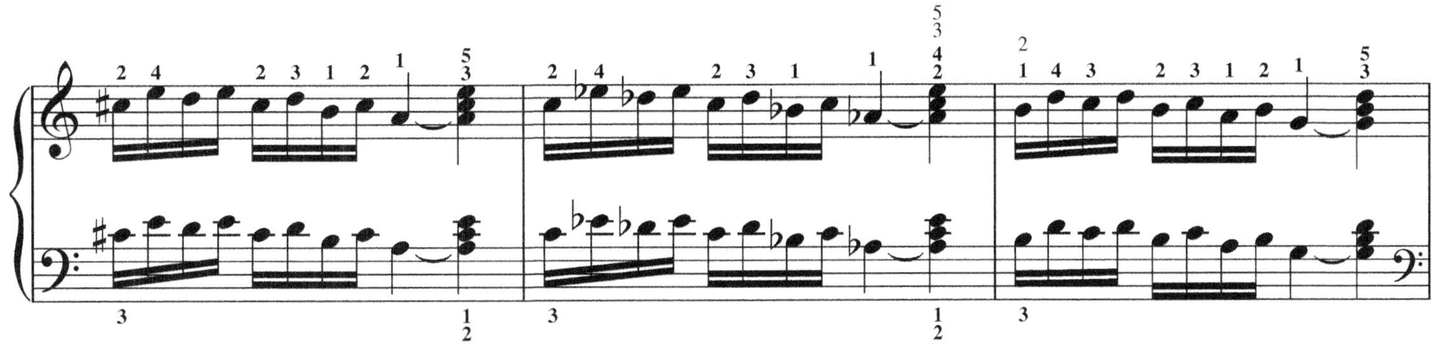

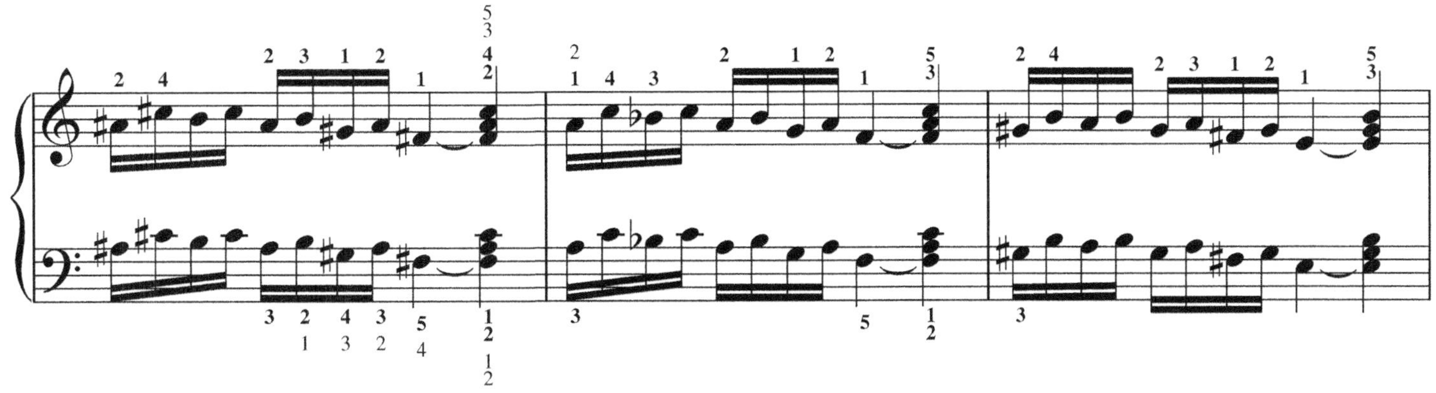

(6b and 6c are rhythmic variations of exercise 6a—choose one and move chromatically or alternate variations in each subsequent key.)

Practice warm-ups 7a–9a also in minor keys. Keep the fifth finger straight, facing toward the keys. Let go of the thumb as soon as it strikes the key and find the point of support in fingers 2–5. Observe the resulting arm motion.

7a
Interval of the third.
7b

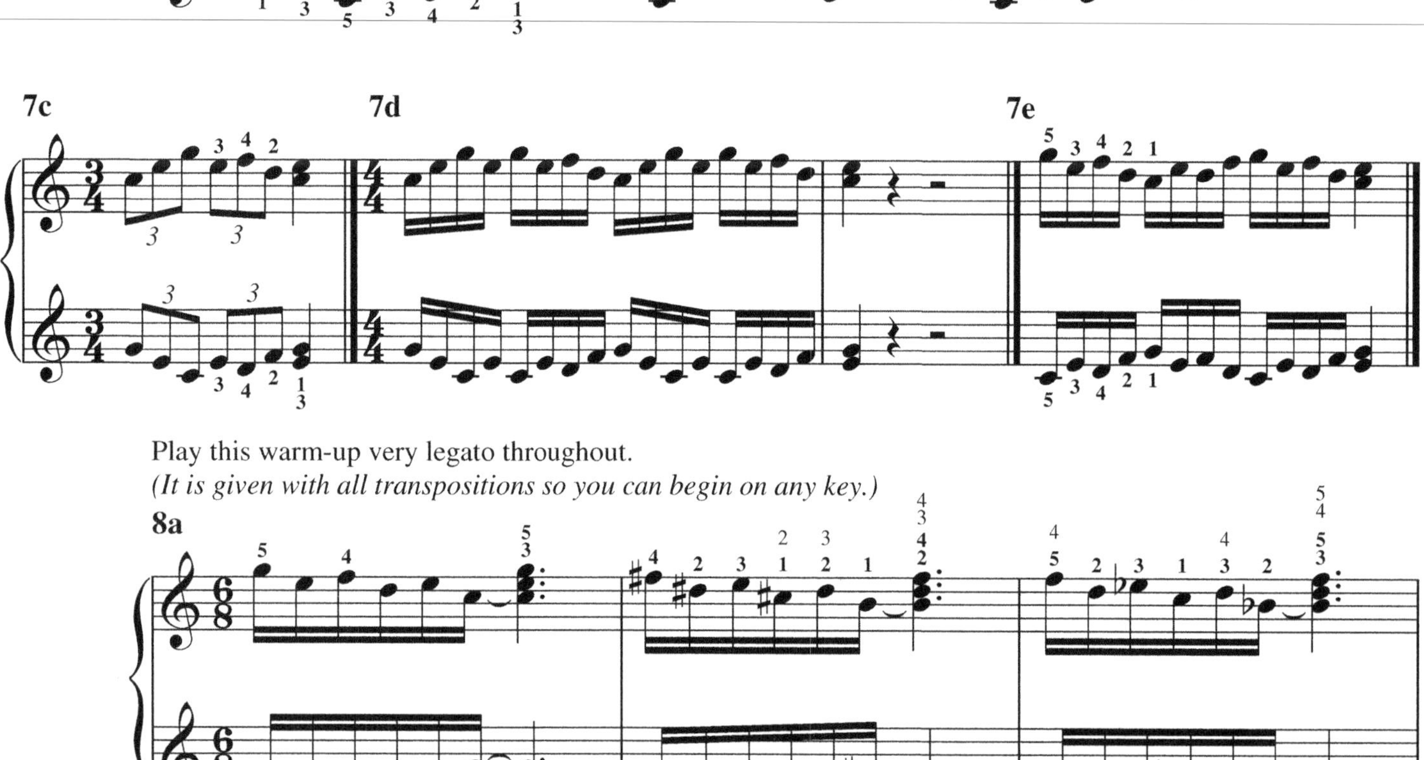
7c
7d
7e
Play this warm-up very legato throughout.
(It is given with all transpositions so you can begin on any key.)
8a

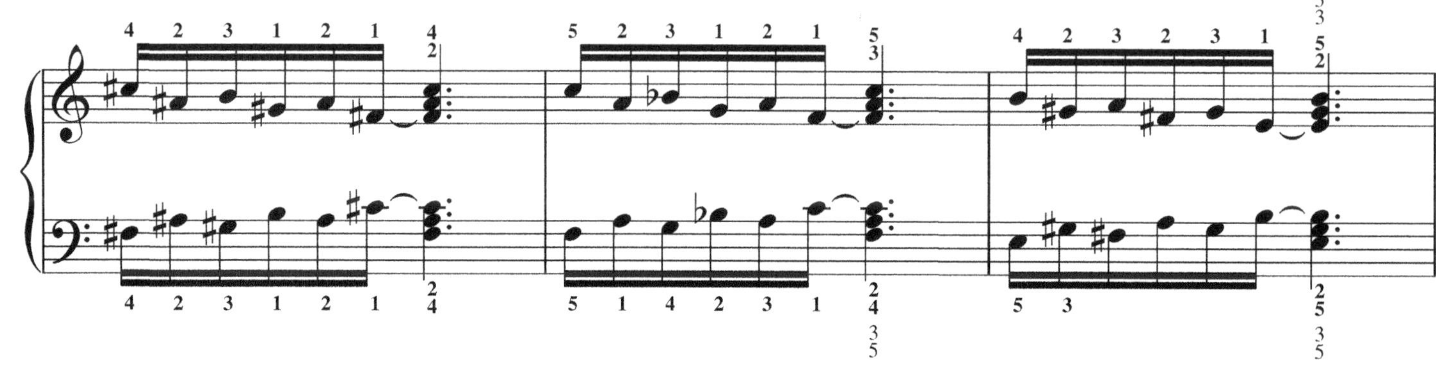

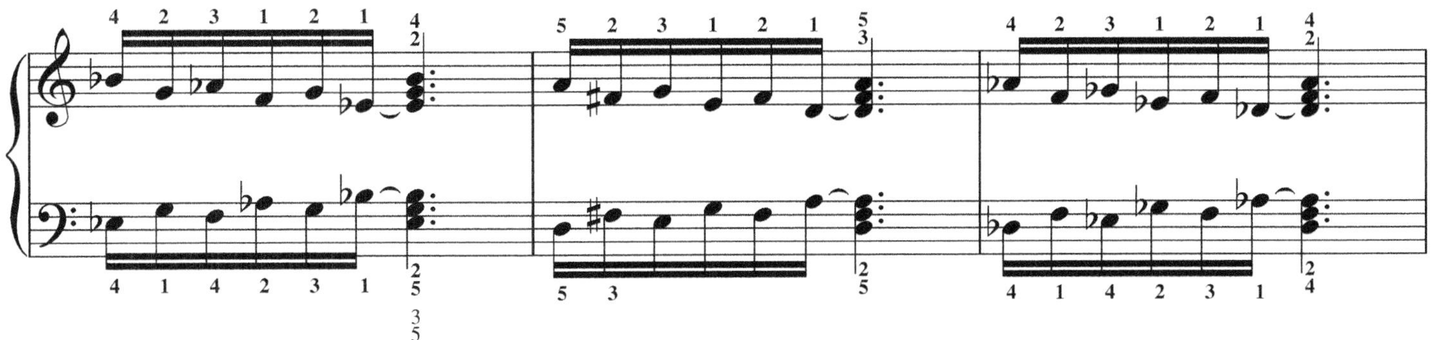

Play with the tip of the thumb on the edge of the keys in a way that allows the fingers to pass over. The arm and hand should remain in a straight line.

Play through warm-ups 9a–14c softly at first, in a moderate tempo, with arm motion; then slightly faster with a firmer sound, less arm motion and more active fingers. *(Finish all exercises in the tonic of each key, as in 9a.)* You can transpose them chromatically in all 12 keys in either ascending or descending order.

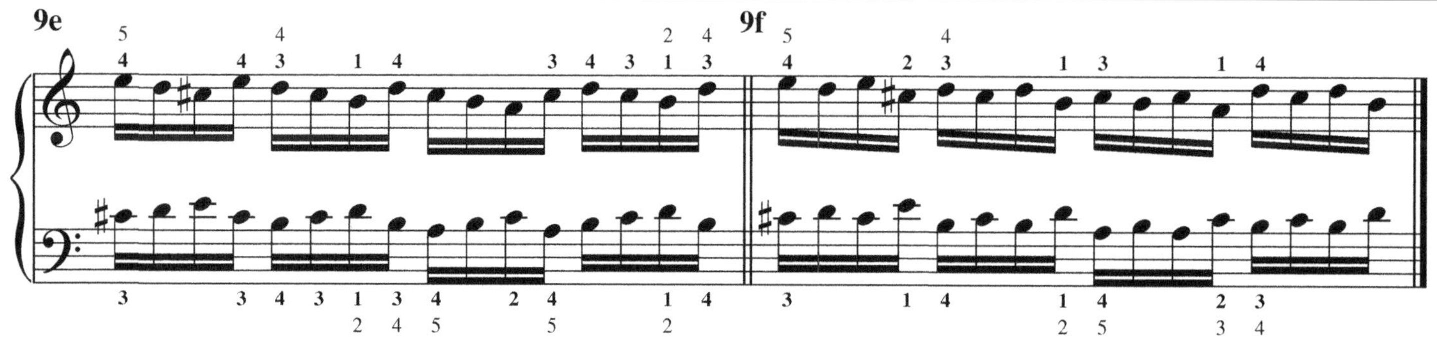

(sample fingering for flat keys)

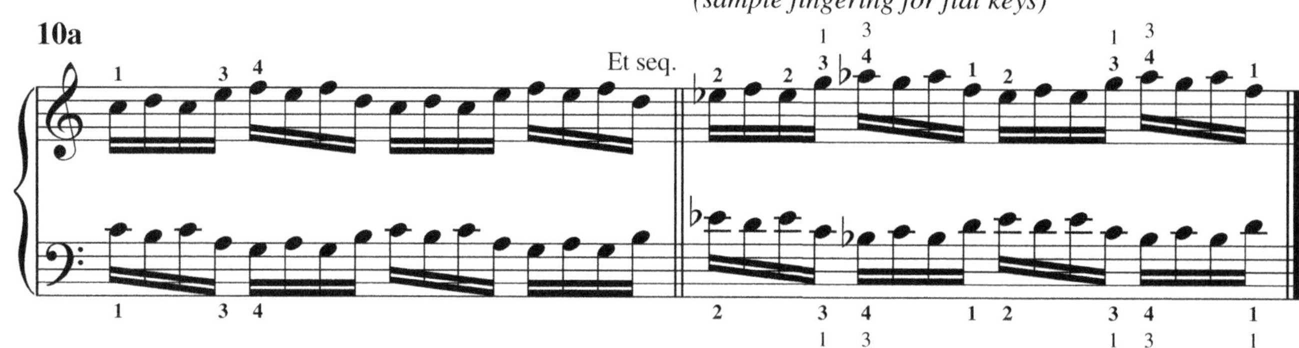

Try transposing exercise 10c chromatically in descending motion with the left hand a minor sixth below the right.

Synthesized warm-ups.

11b

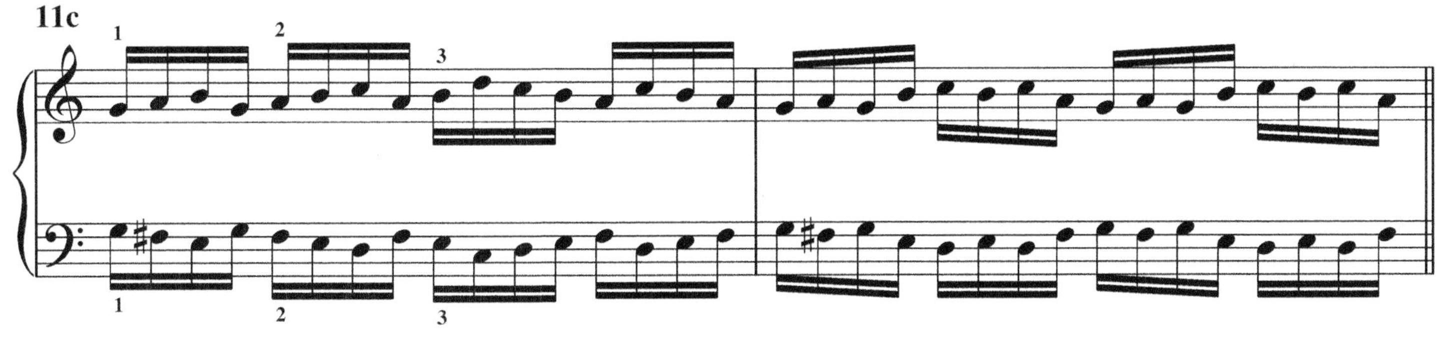
11c

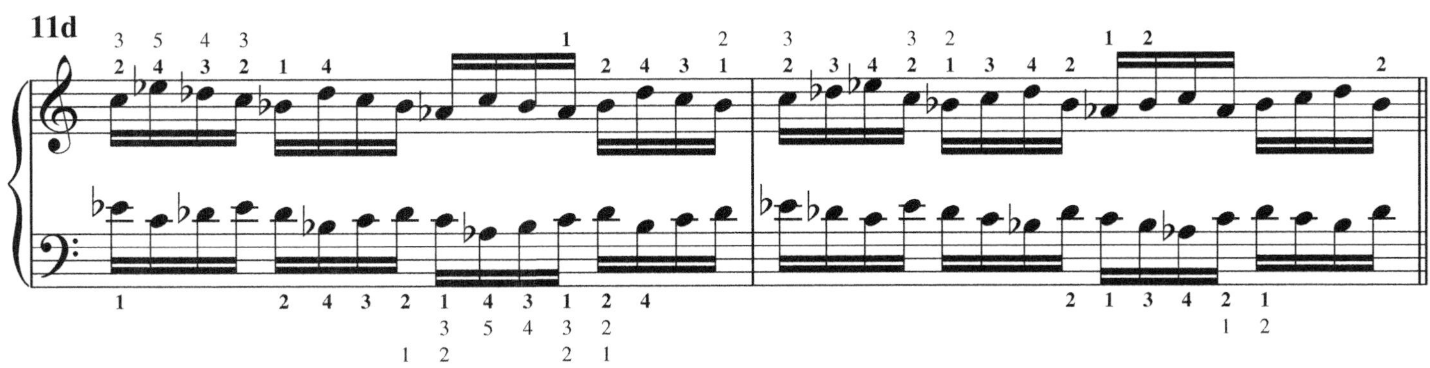
11d

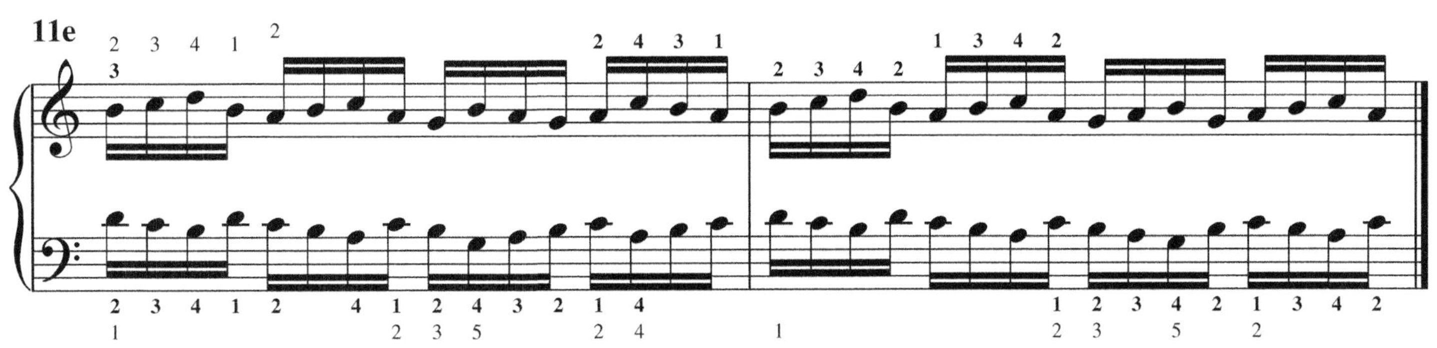
11e

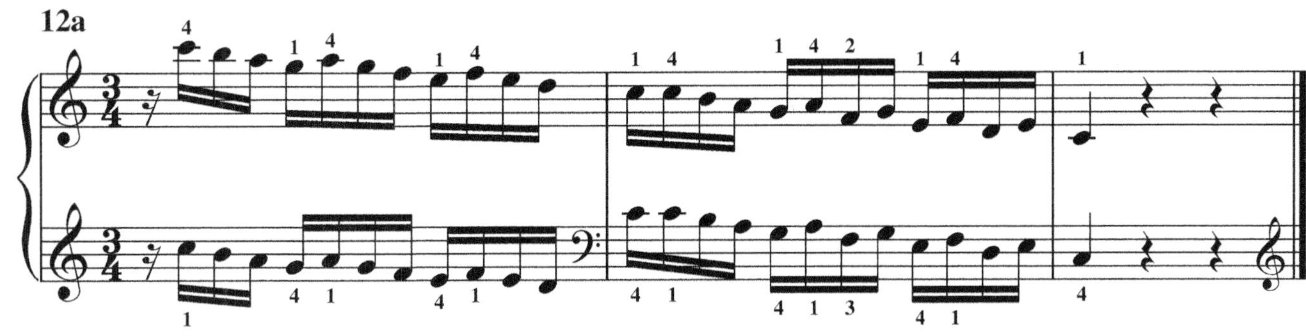
12a

12b

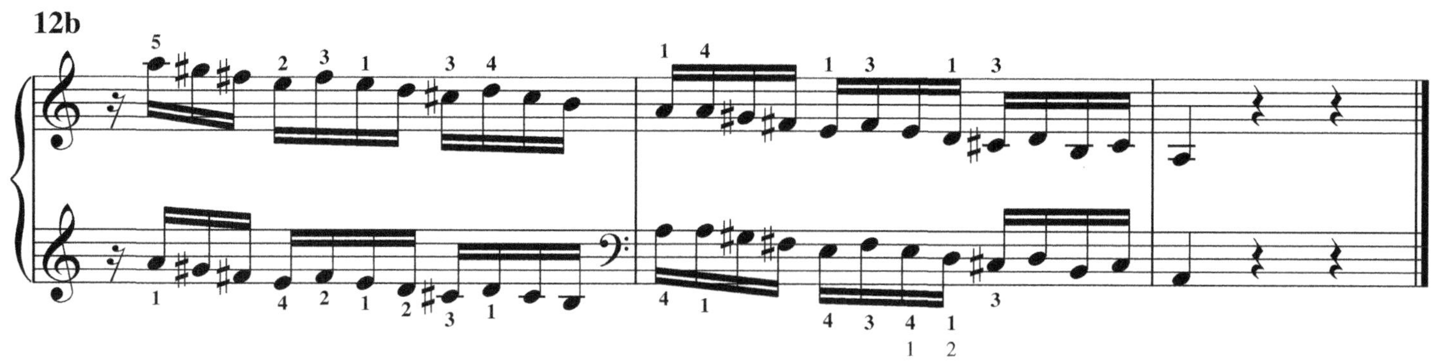

13a

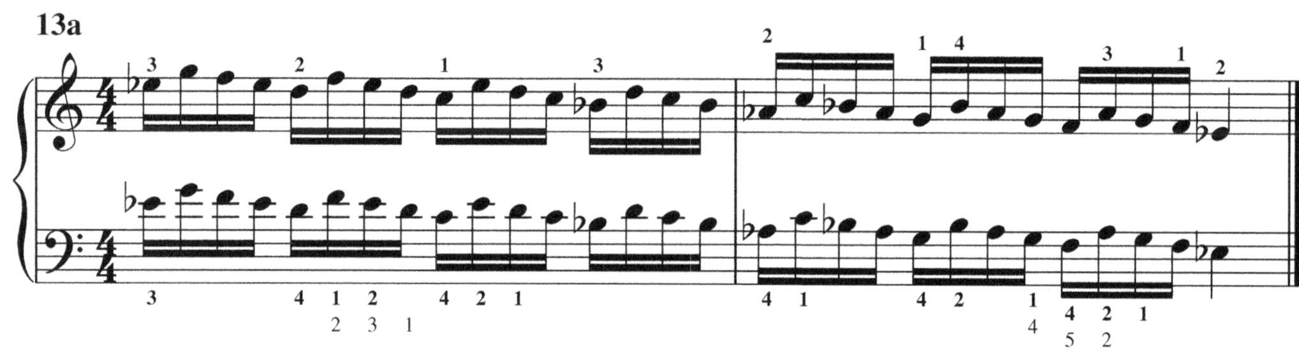

13b

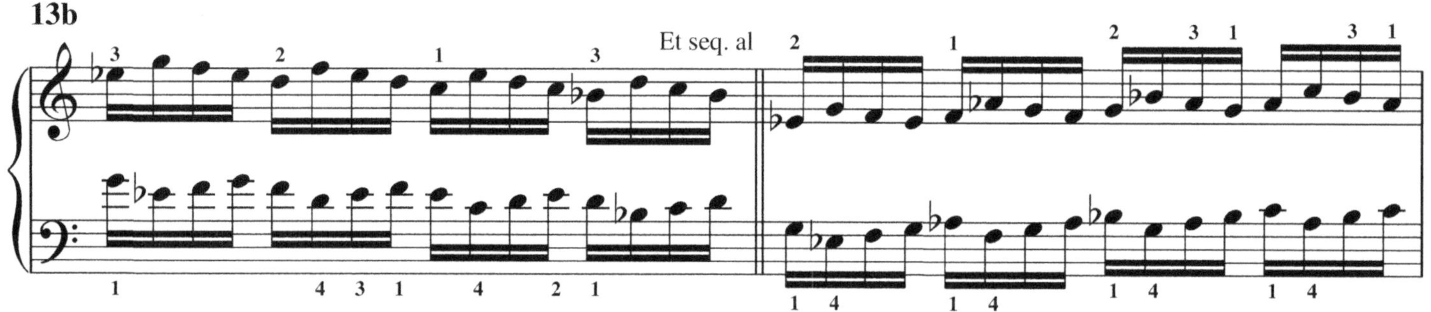

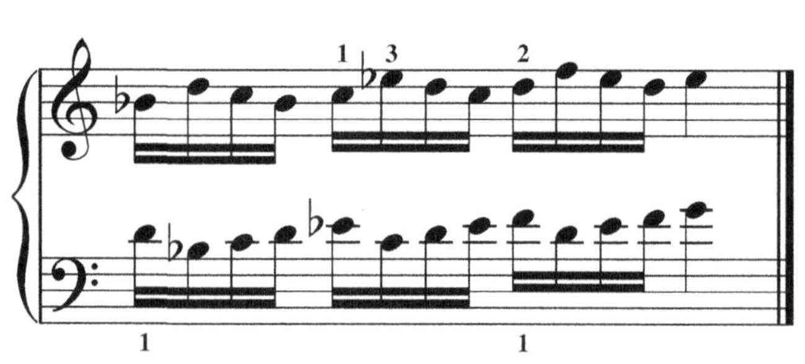

Trill preparation.

14a

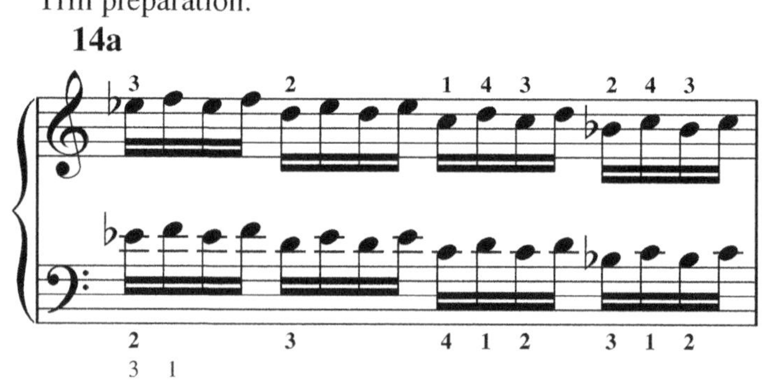

Synthesized warm-ups.

14b *(sample fingering for flat-key scale)*

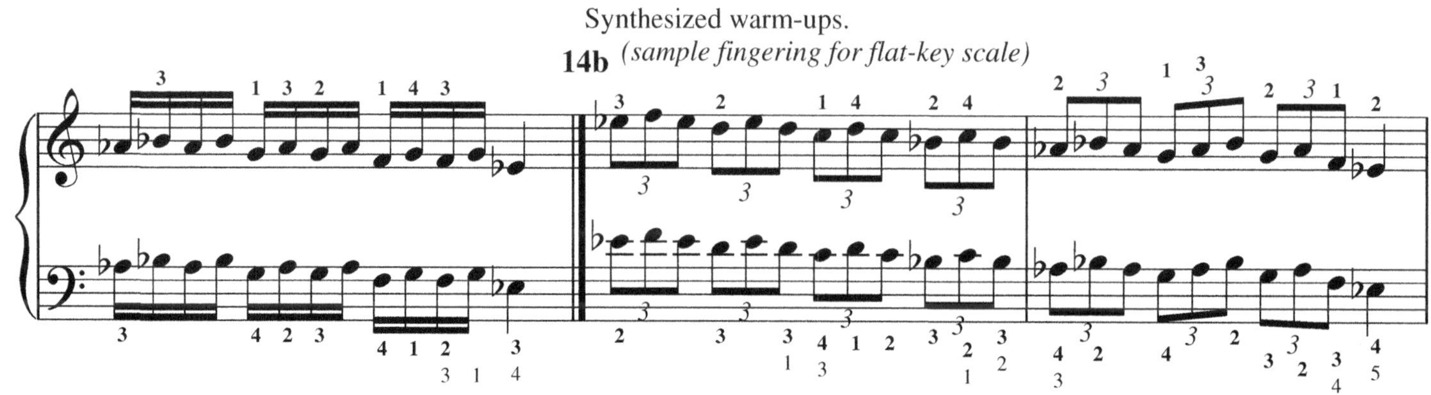

14c
Warm-ups in triplets.
15a
15b

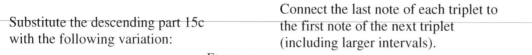

Substitute the descending part 15c with the following variation:

Connect the last note of each triplet to the first note of the next triplet (including larger intervals).

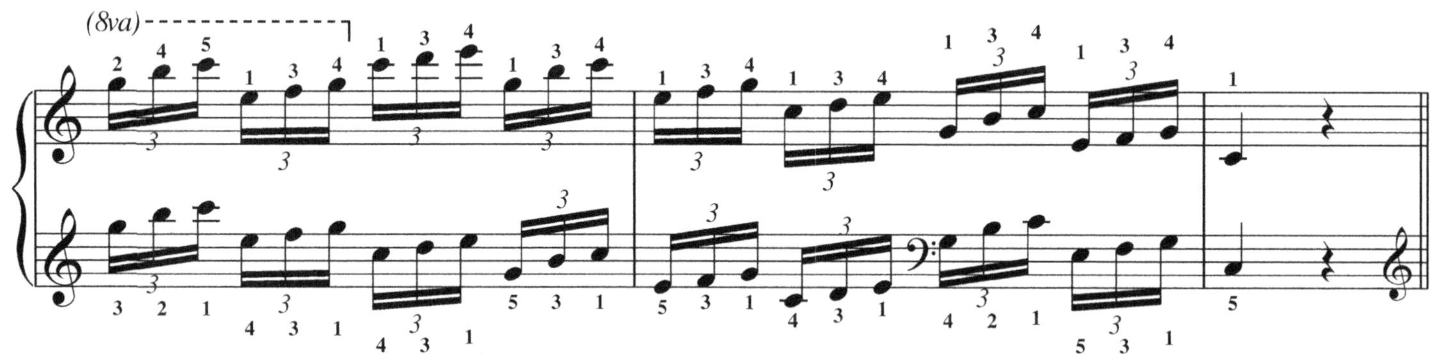

Substitute the descending part of 15e with the following variation:

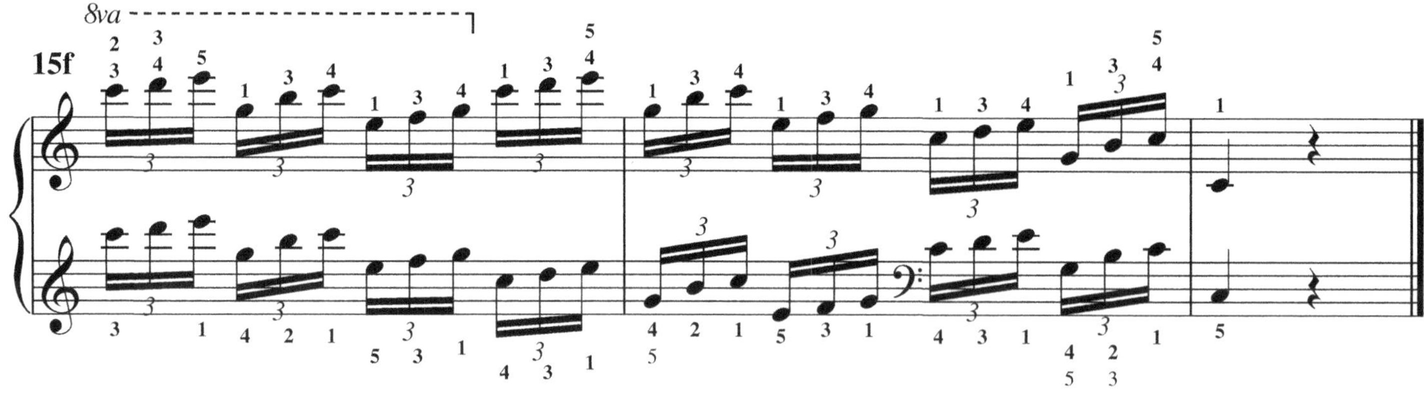

Fingerings of "elision." Keep the arm and hand aligned. The fingers should be active and close to the keys.

16b

16c

17a

(Same as 17a but moving chromatically with each repetition of the motive.)

17b

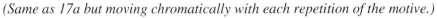

You can exchange the parallel and contrary variations of 17d and e in the ascending and descending motion.

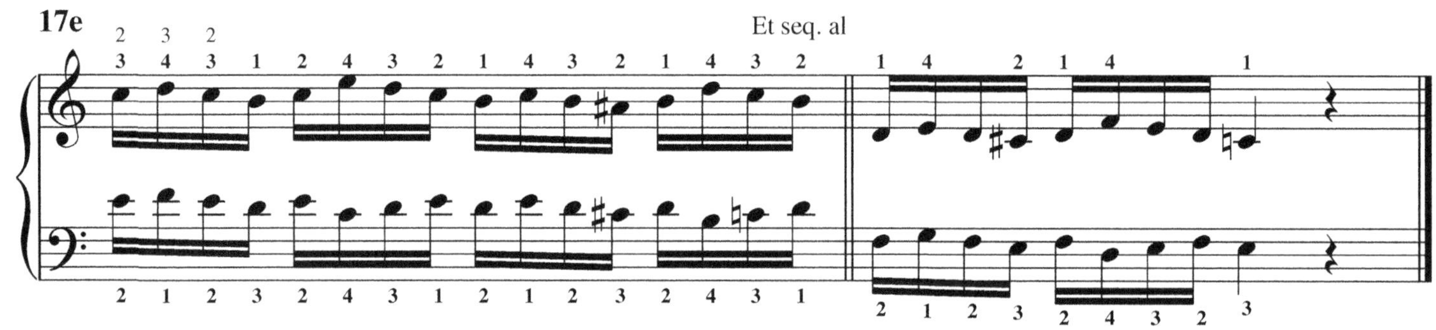

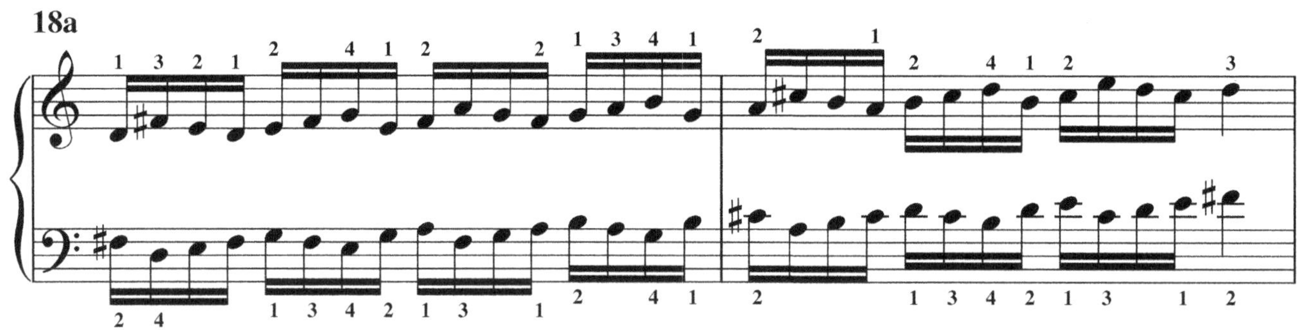

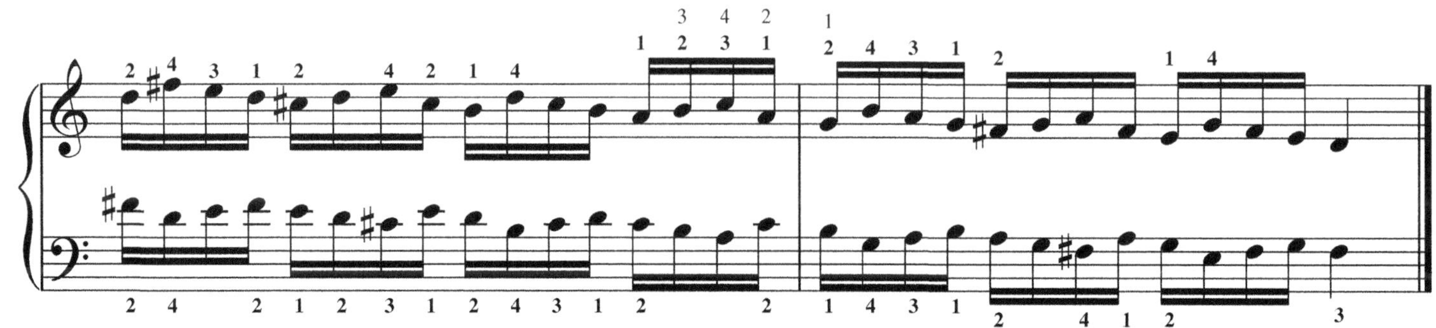

(Same as 18b but moving chromatically. Apply the same to 18d and e.)

The fingering in between the staffs can be used by both hands.

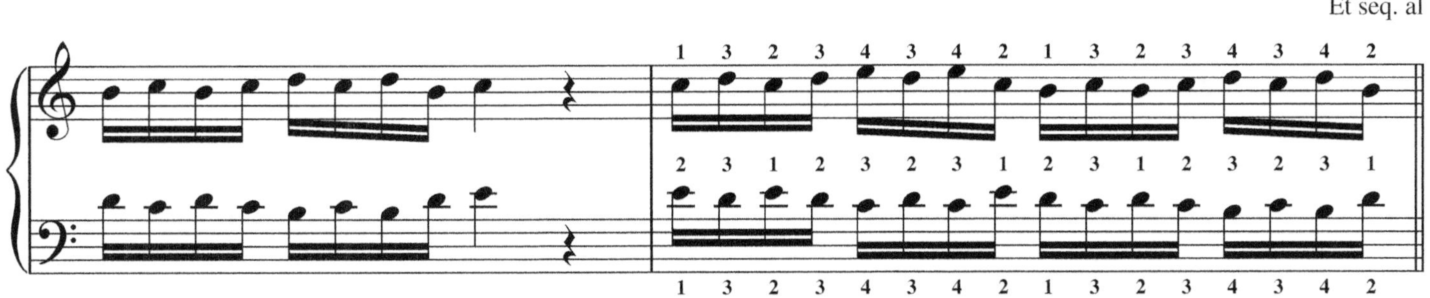

(Same as 18f but moving chromatically.)

The hand-arm alignment remains the same throughout.

19a

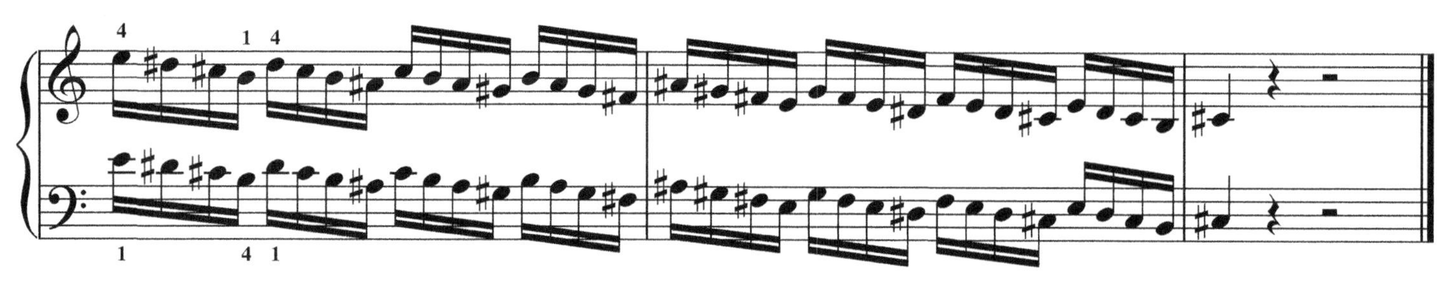

19b

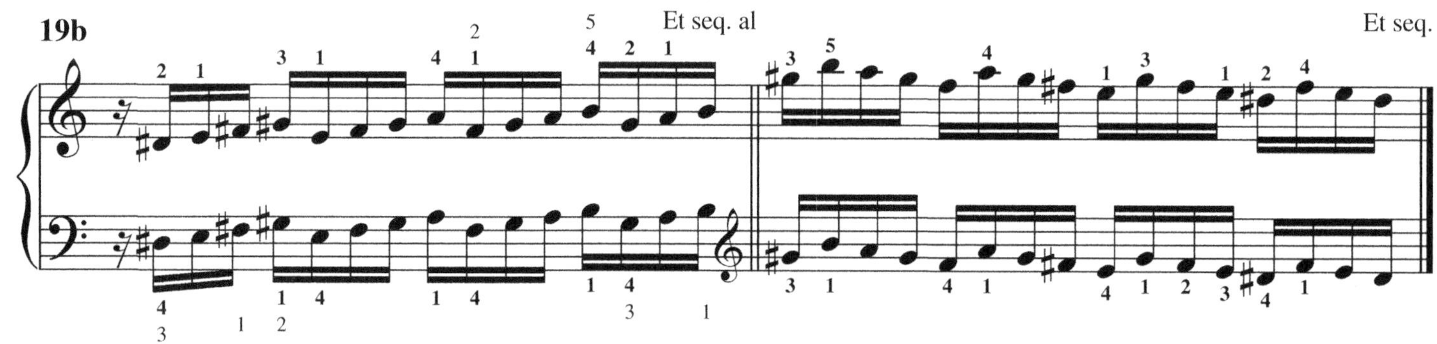

Interval of the fourth.

20a

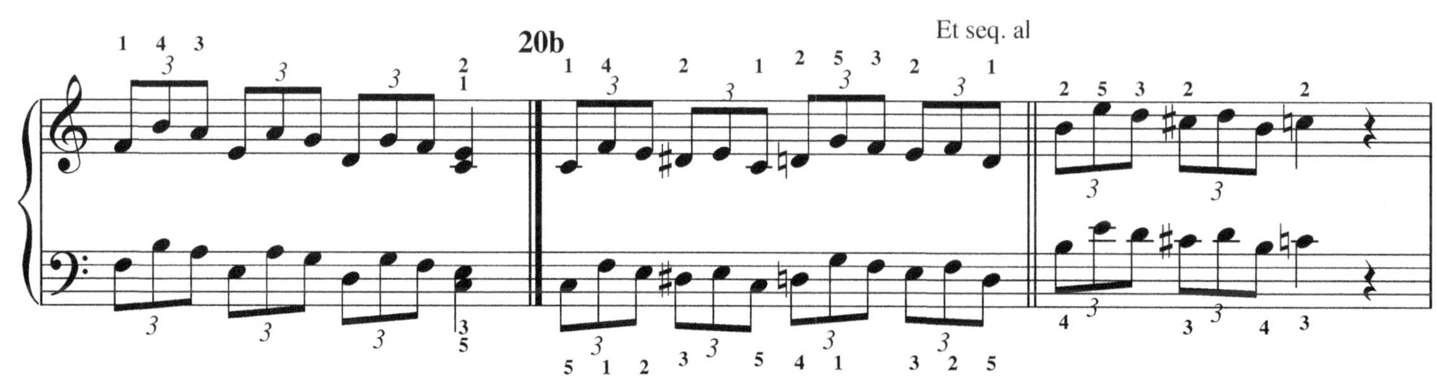

(Same as 20b but without chromatic notes.)
Et seq. al
20c
Et seq. (as in 20b).
Interval of the sixth.
21a
Et seq. al
21b
(Ending similar to 21a.)
21c
Et seq.
Et seq. al

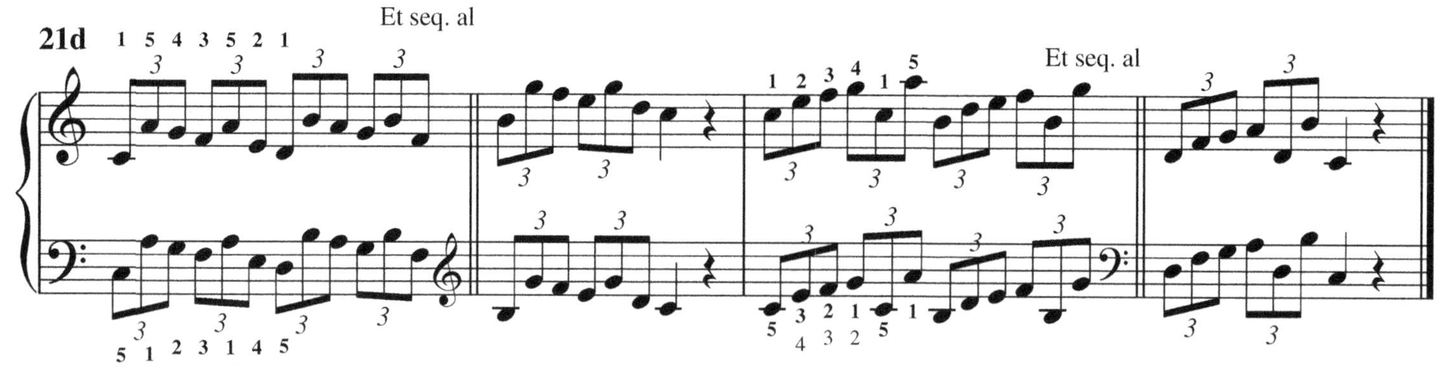

Interval of the octave.

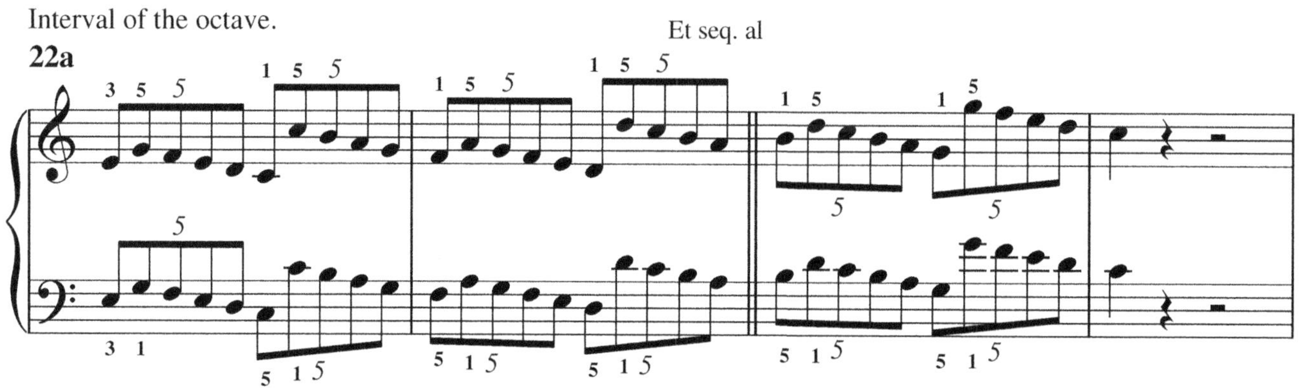

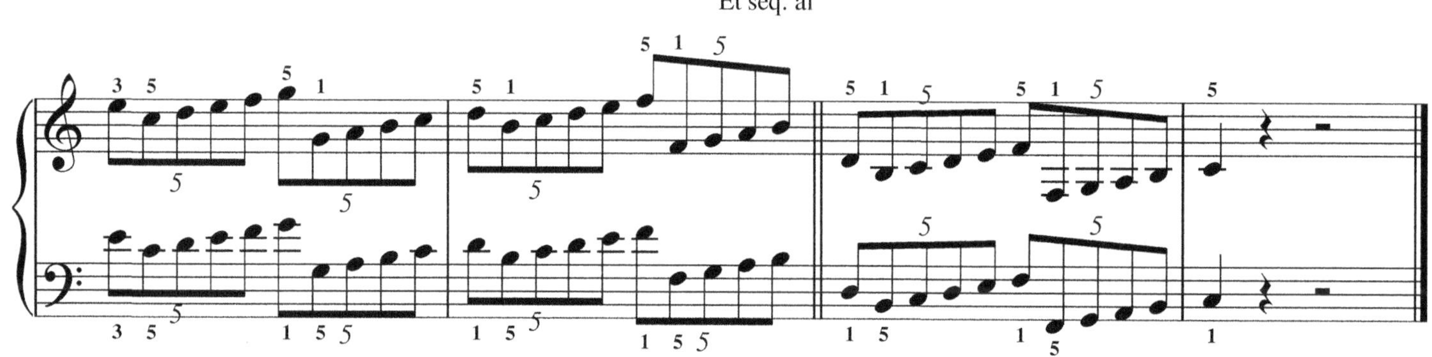

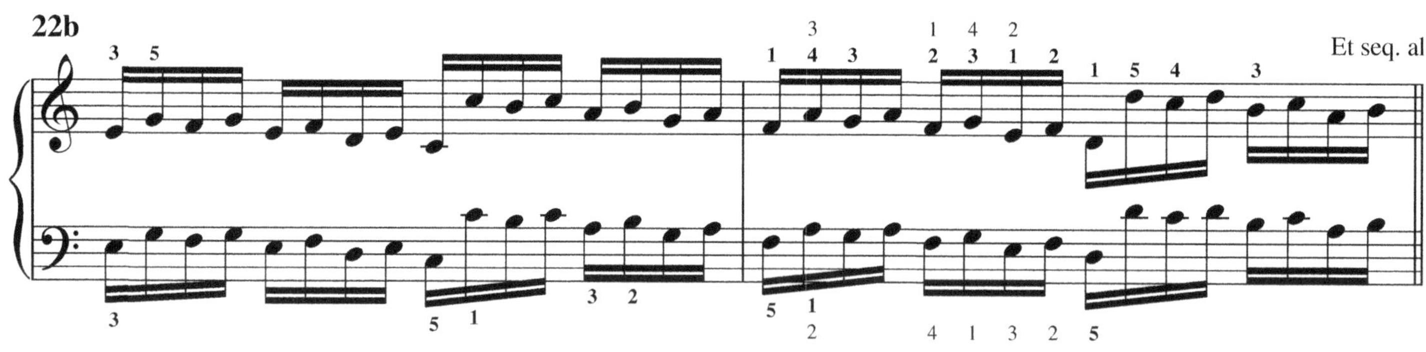

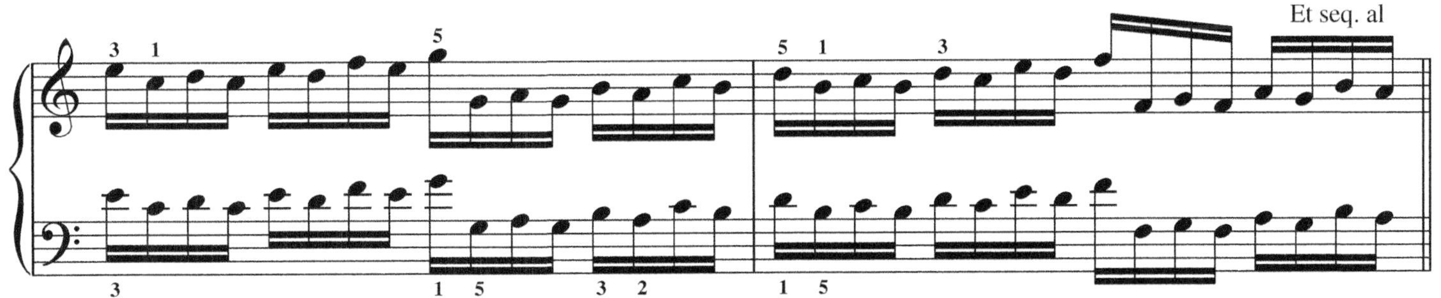

Interval of the tenth. Reach the tenth with a lateral shift of the arm.
Shift back to the thumb in the descending intervals.

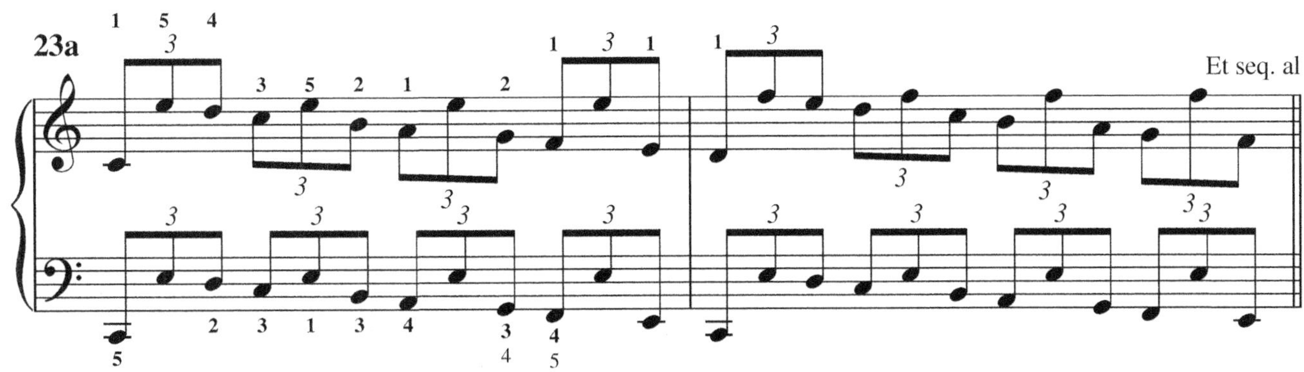

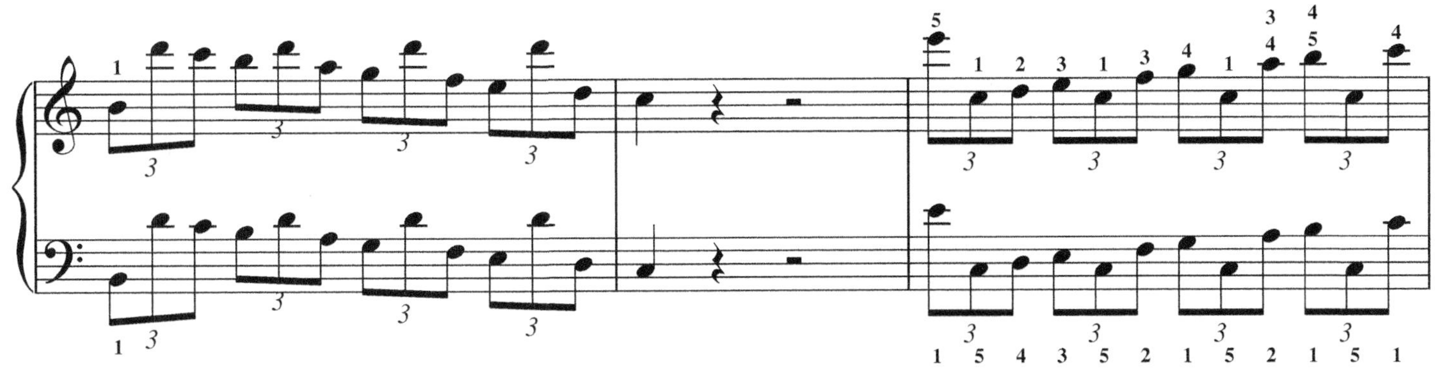

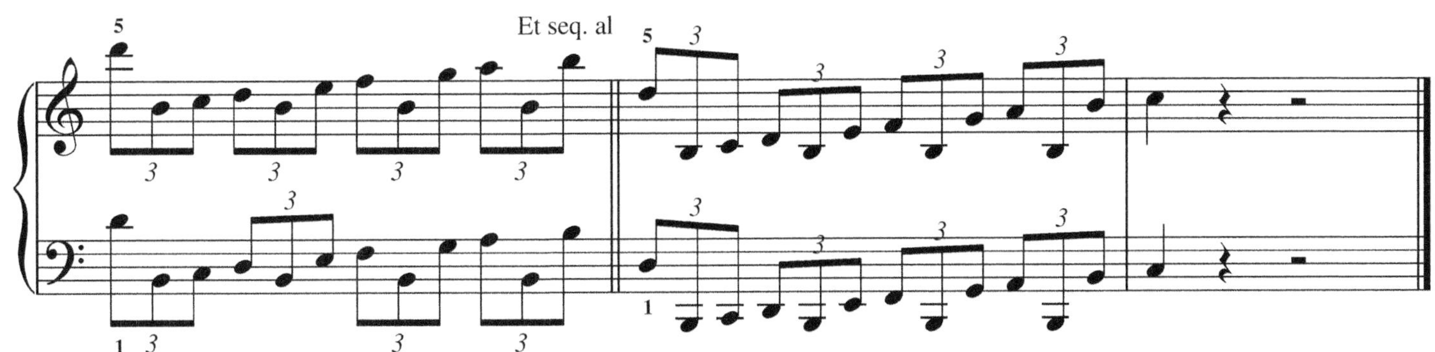

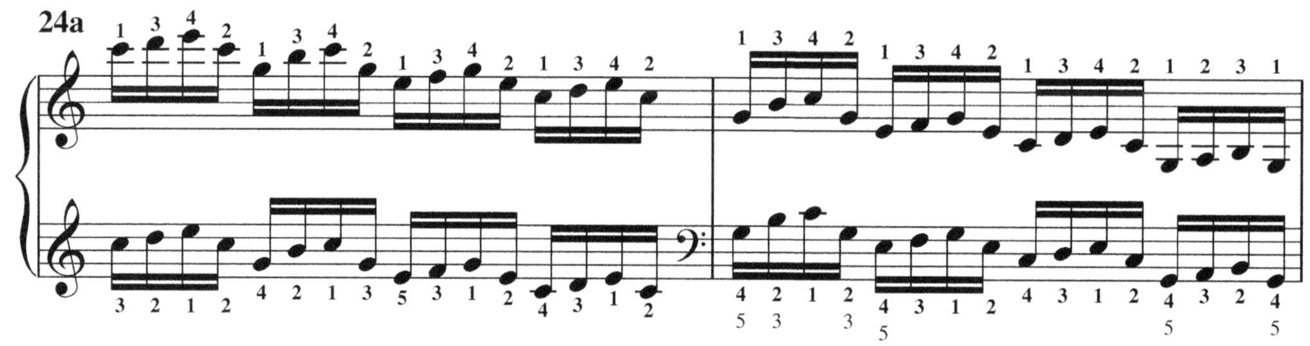

Keep thumb in proper position to allow the fingers to pass over.

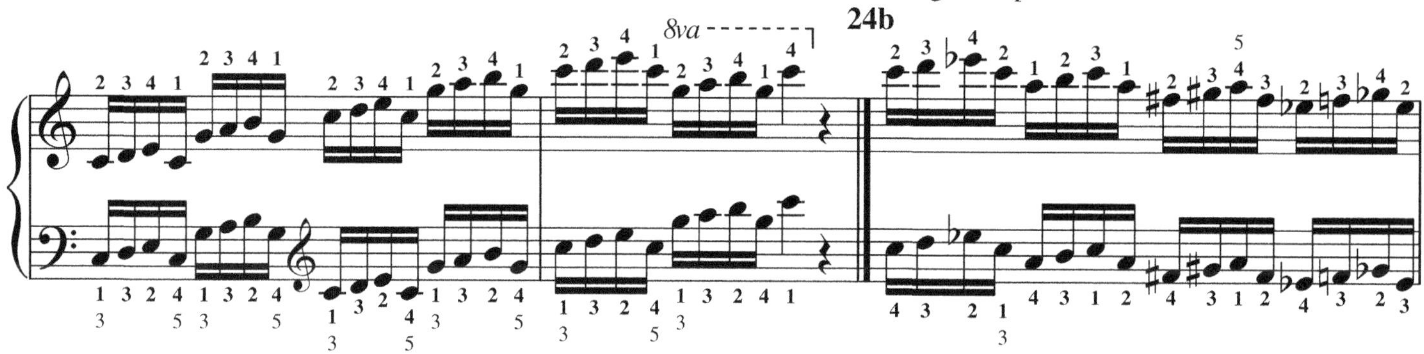

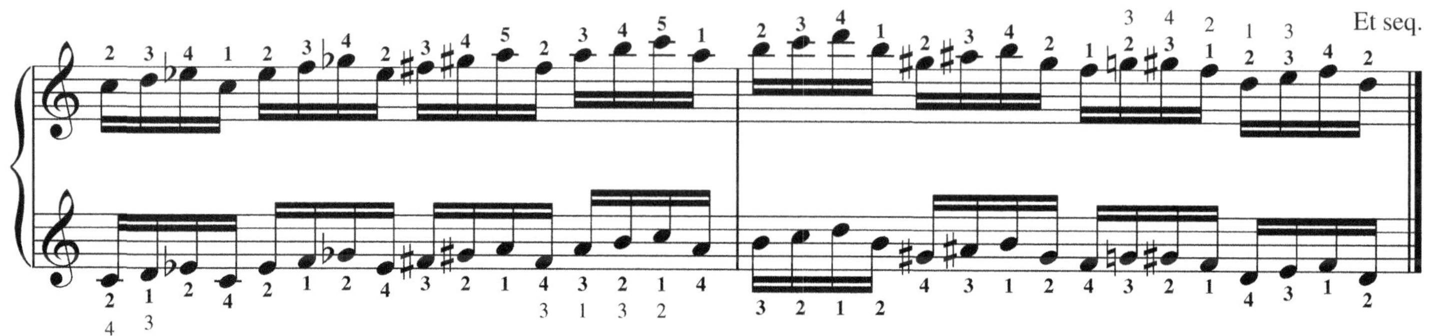

Finger substitution on the same note.

The thumb "renews" the hand. Note that it stays on the keys the least of all the fingers.

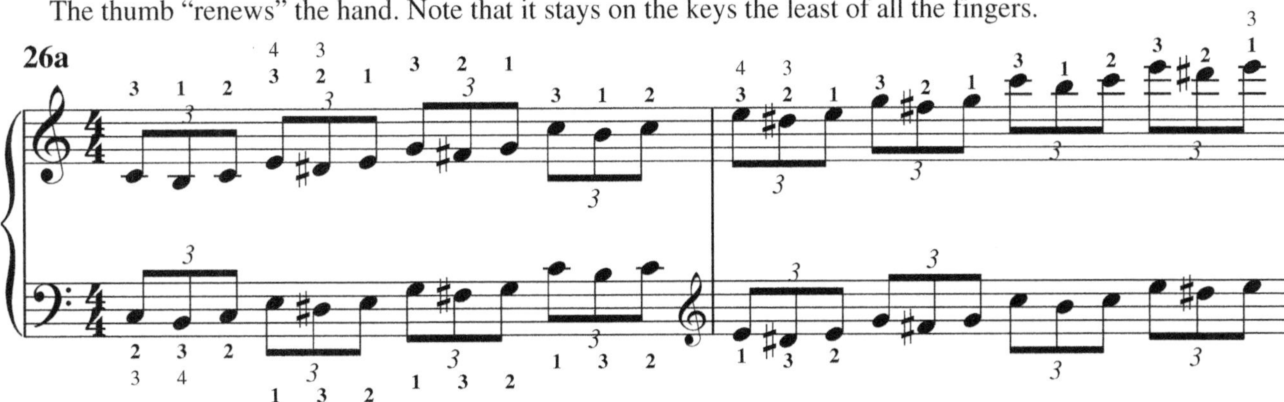

Play the following warm-up with active fingers and a legato touch. Also play in various tempos and dynamics.

26b

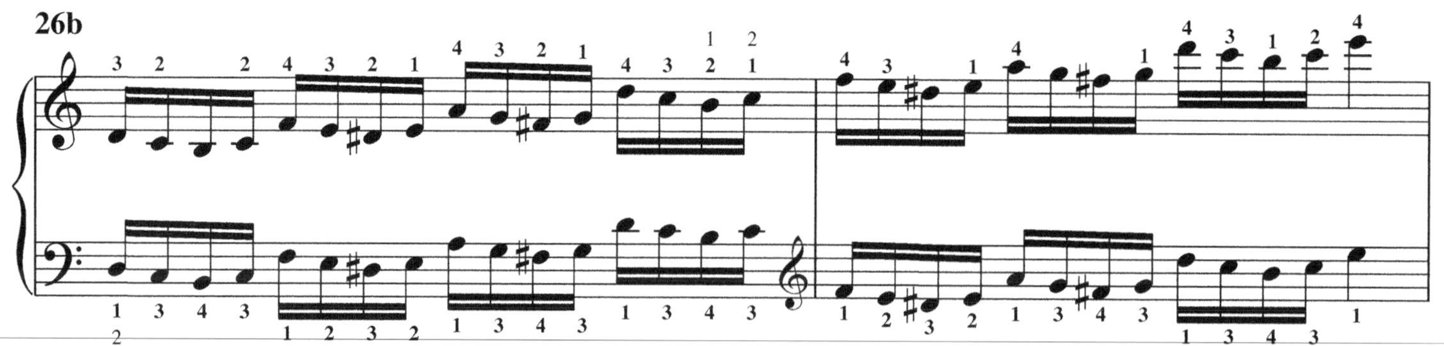

27a

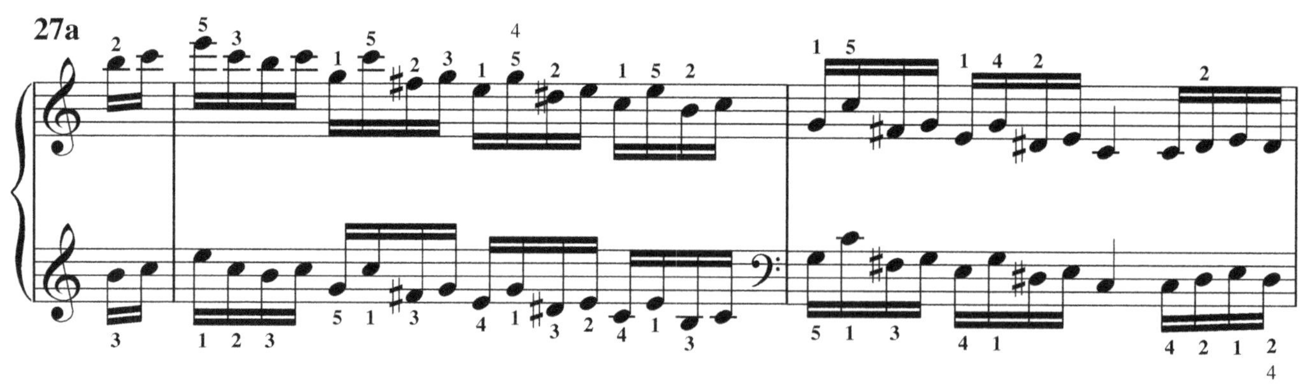

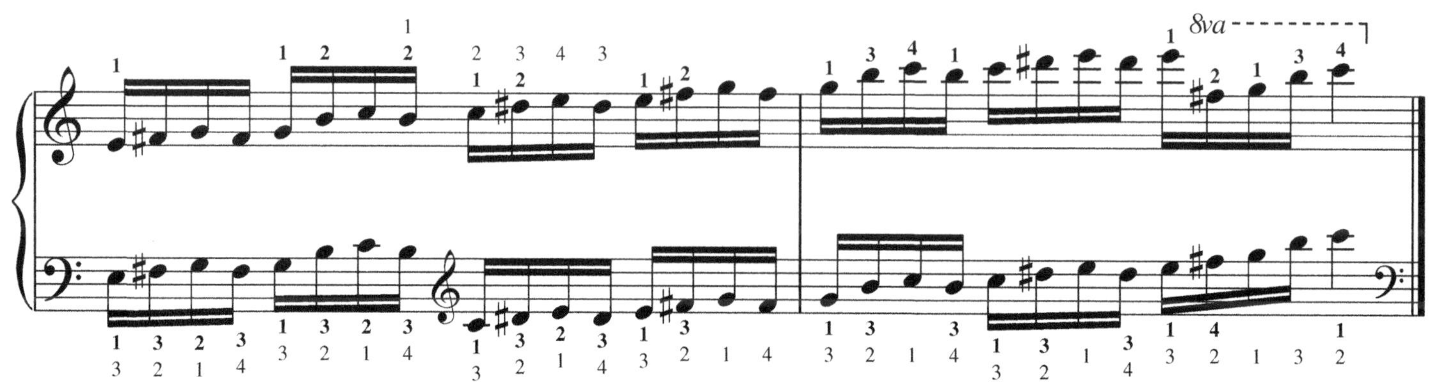

27b
8va
(8va)
The thumb acts as a pivot over which the other fingers pass.
28
Changing fingers on the same key.
29a
Et seq.

Allow the arm to "walk over" fingers 2-3-4.
29b
Et seq.
Find the point of support in fingers 3-4-5.
30a
8va
Reach back for the thumb on the way down.
(8va)

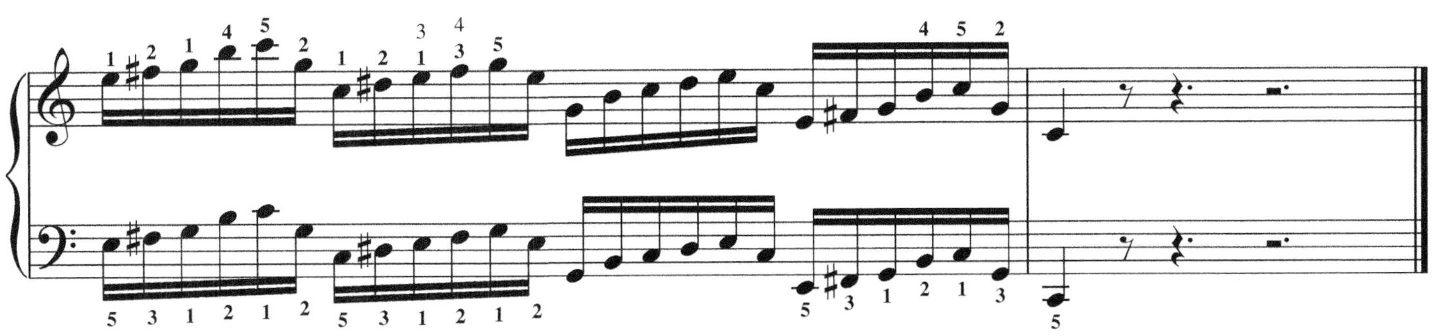

30b

(End as in 30a.)

Reach for the top notes and accent them lightly.

31

Et seq.

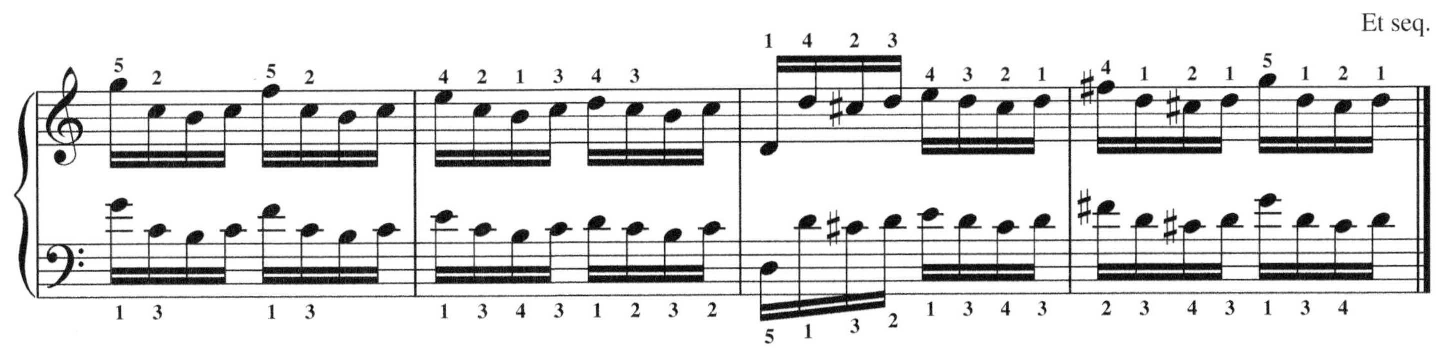

Developing evenness. Teach the thumb to pass under the fingers and the hand over the thumb.

32a

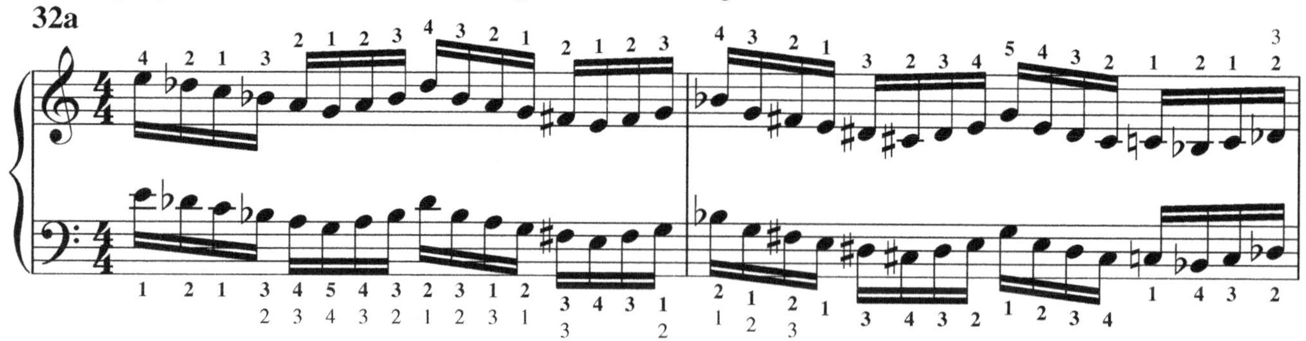

32b

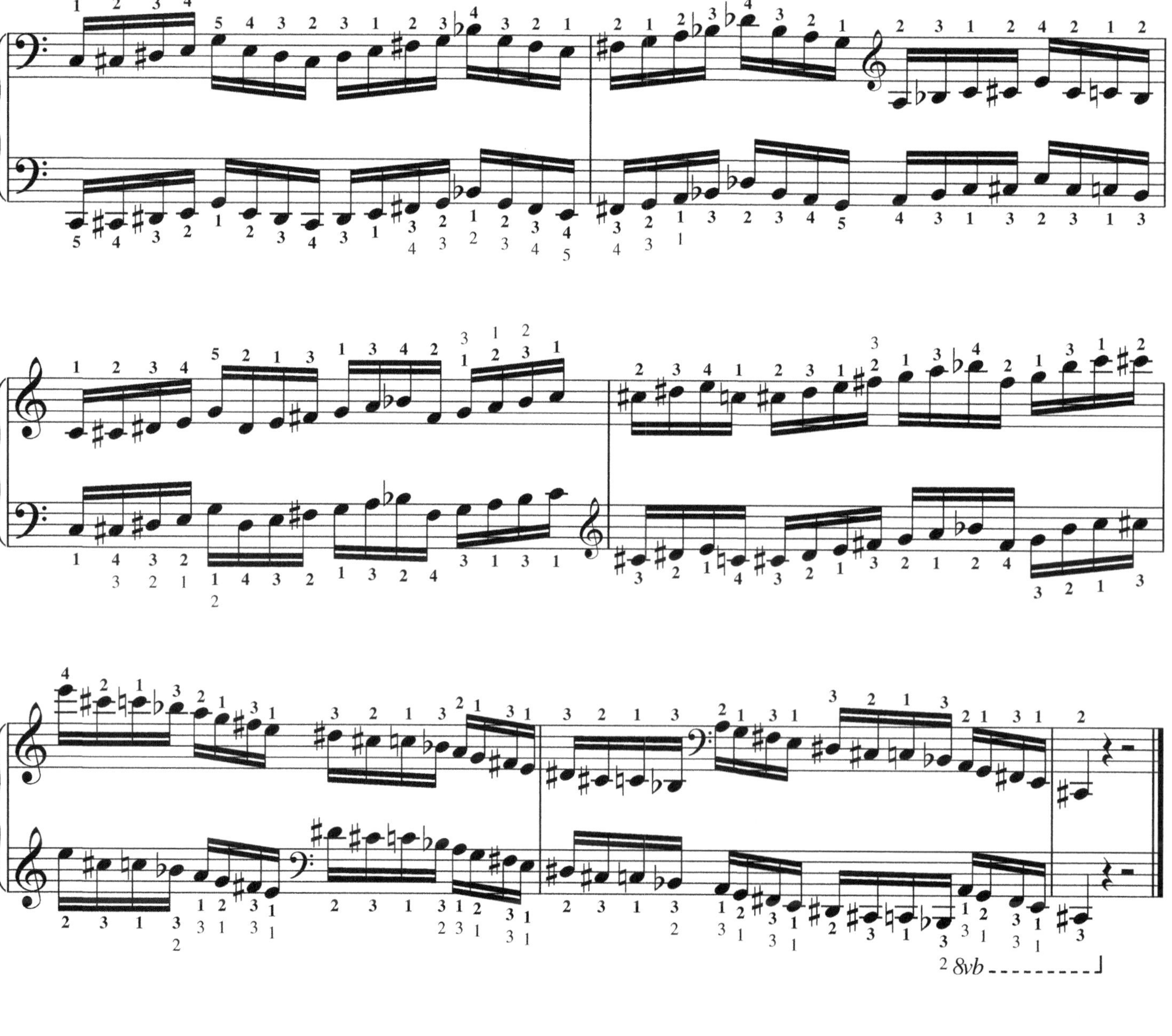

8vb

The entire torso is supported by the hand. Maintain a feeling of connection to the entire arm and upper body with fingers 2-3-4-5. Exercises 30c–e can also be performed in ascending order and chromatically (as in 30b).

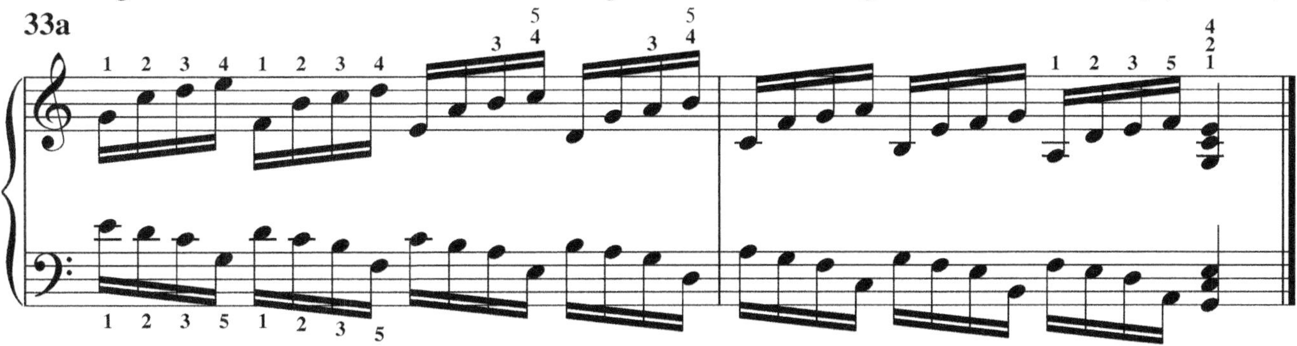

The thumb stays the least on the keys.

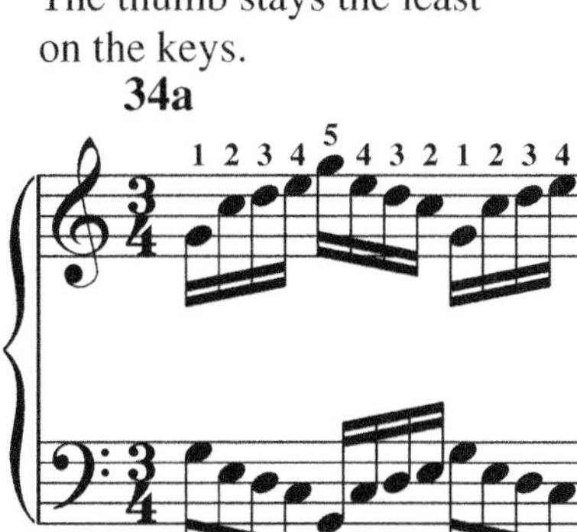

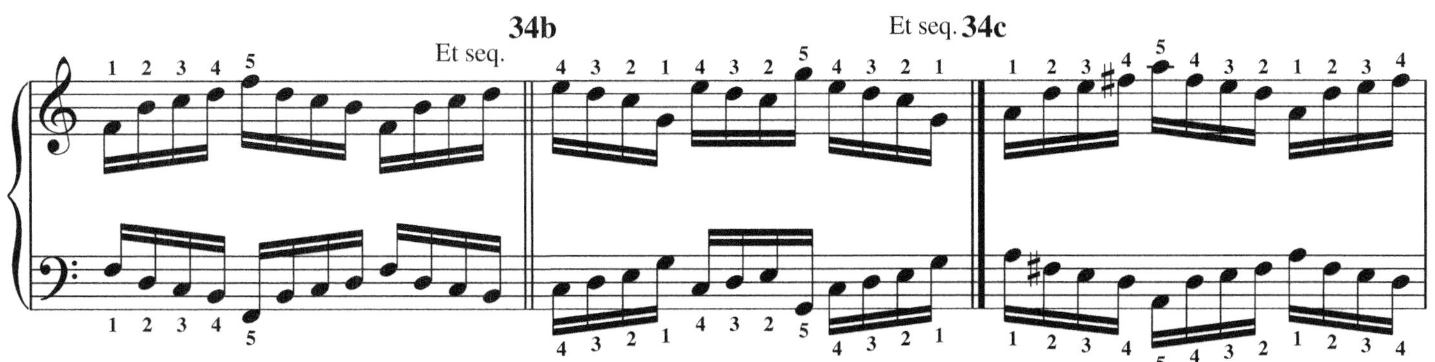

Continue the pattern without interruption in the following positions:

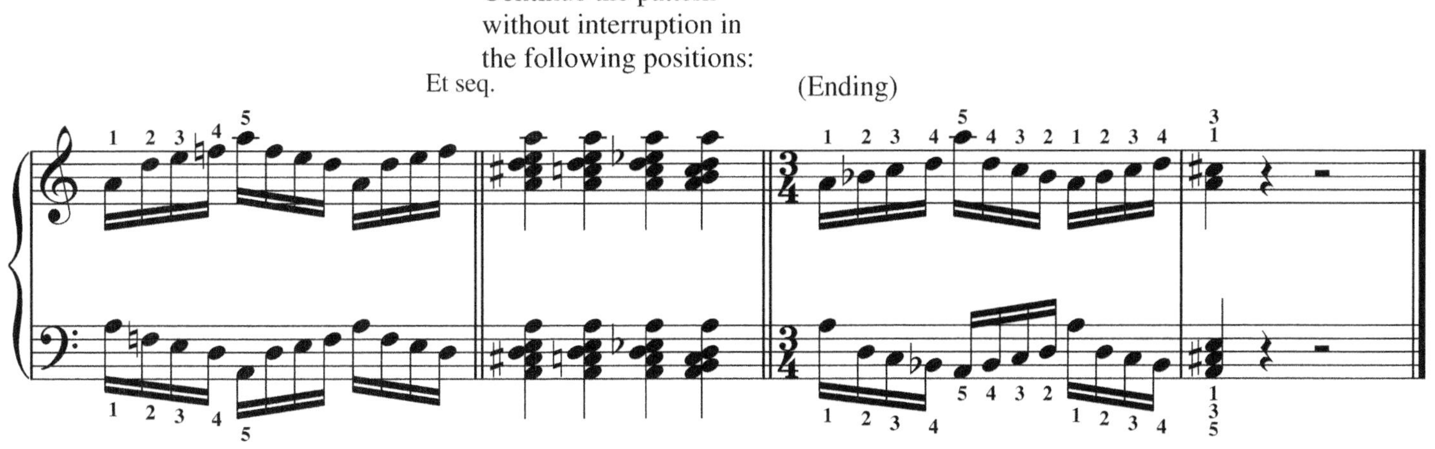

(Follow the chord progression of 34c.)

34d

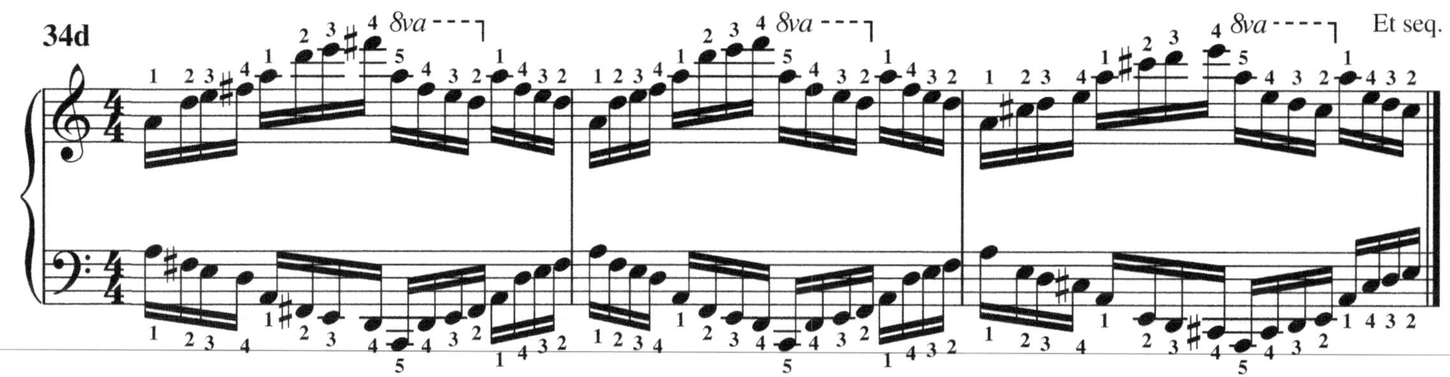

Section B–Scales

Preparatory warm-ups.

1a

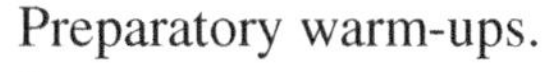

1b

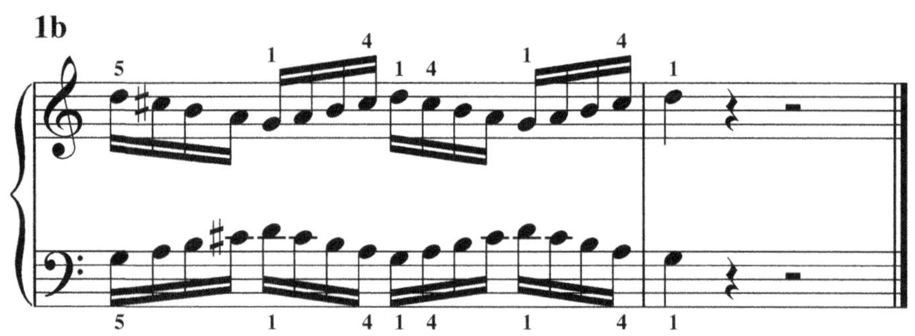

2a

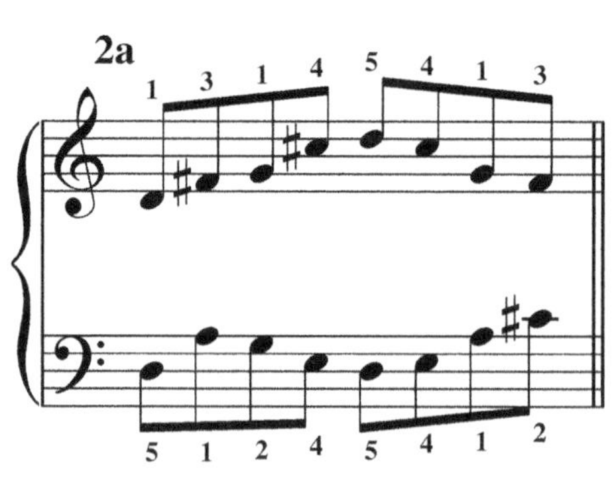

2b

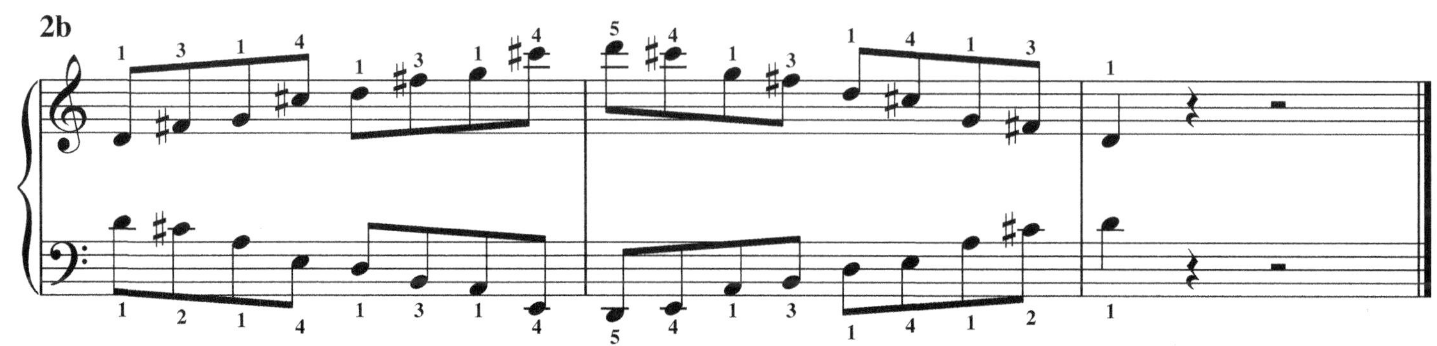

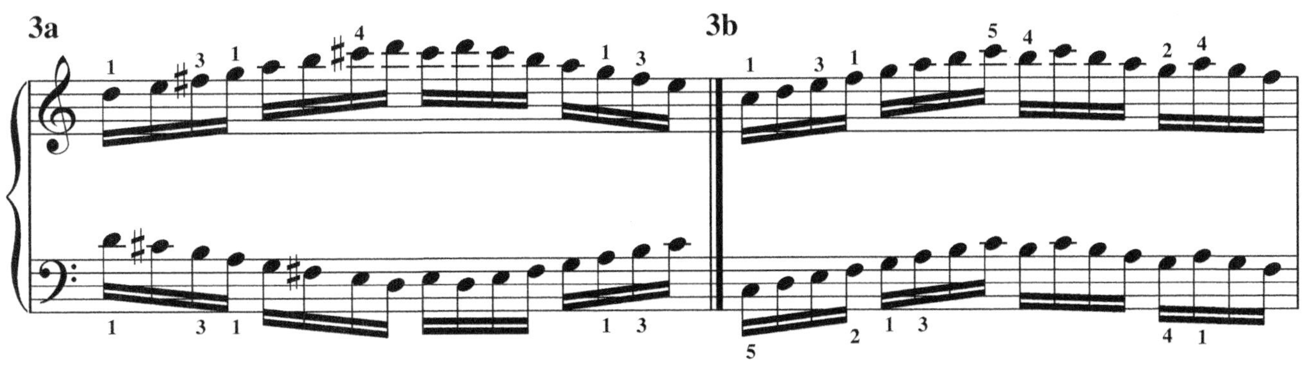

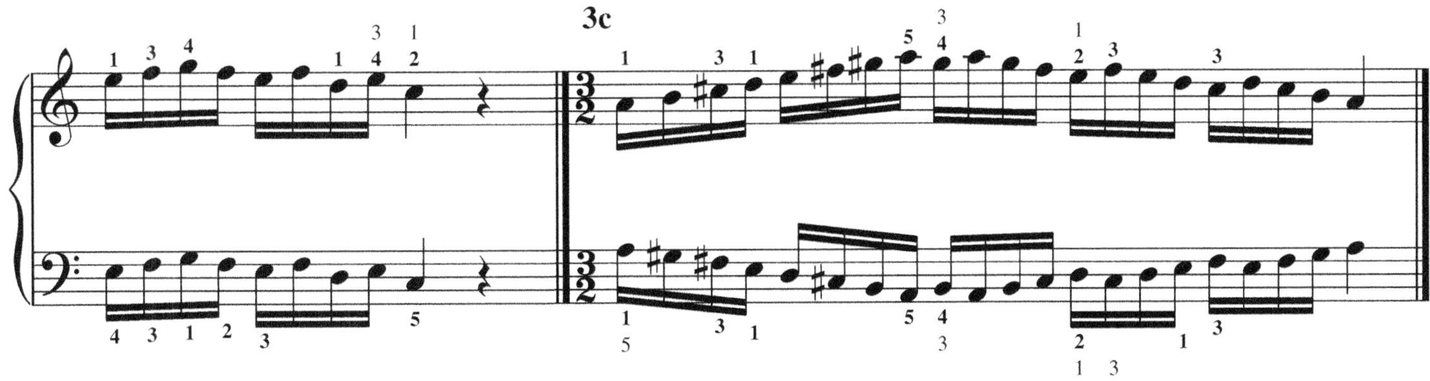

(Keep alternating 4a and b in each subsequent transposition.)

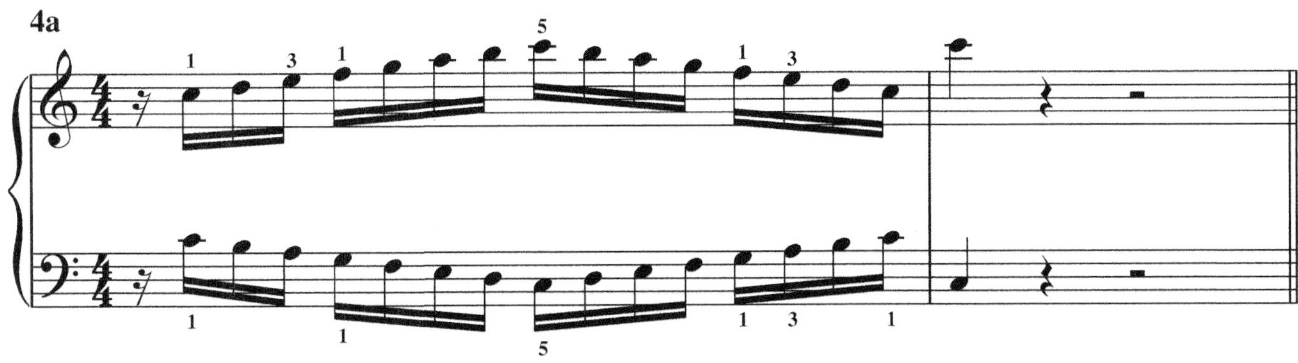

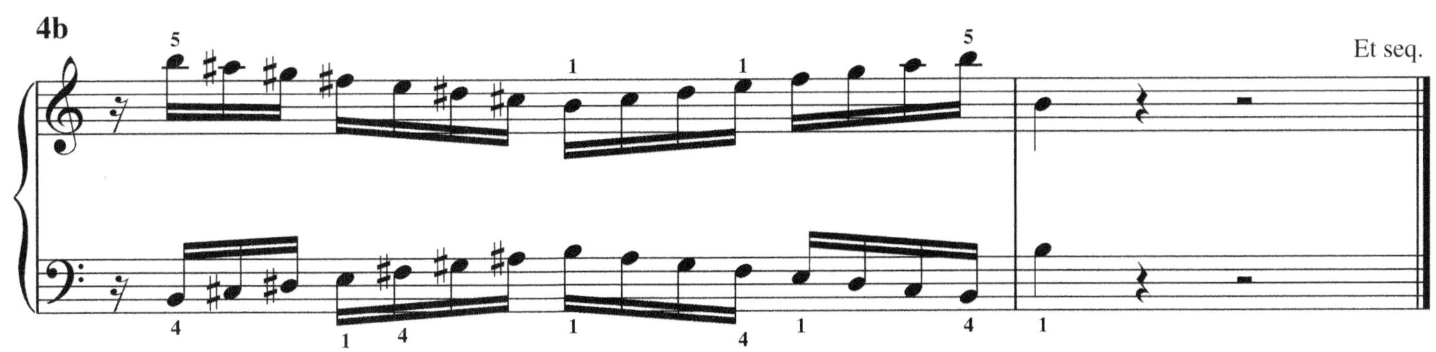

Continuous scale sequences.

5a

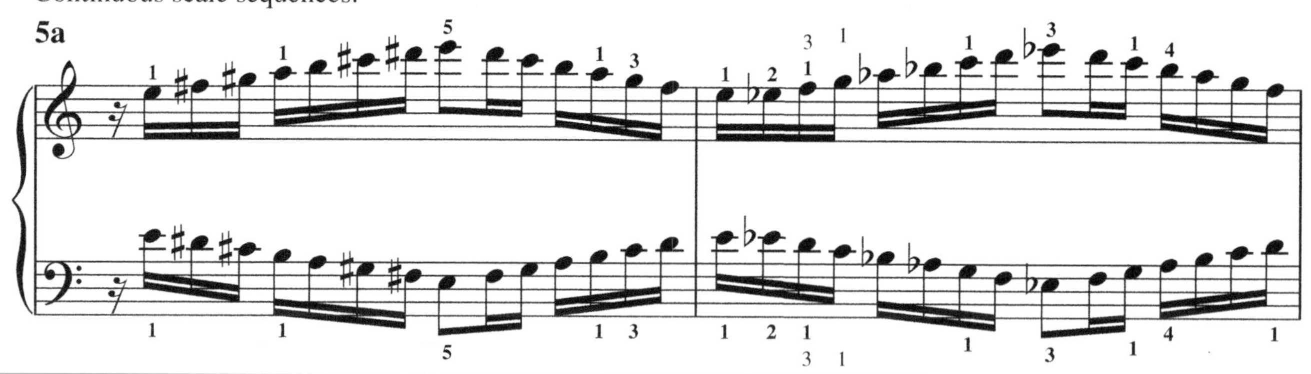

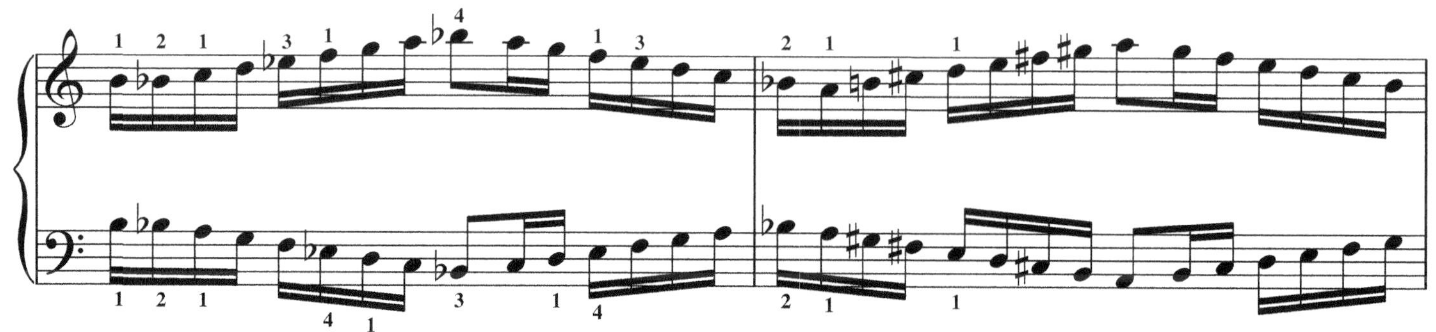

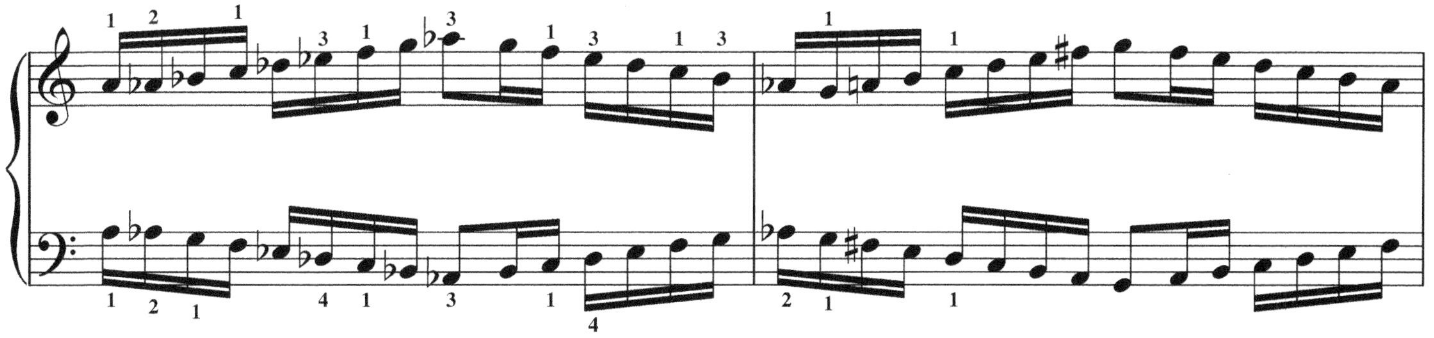

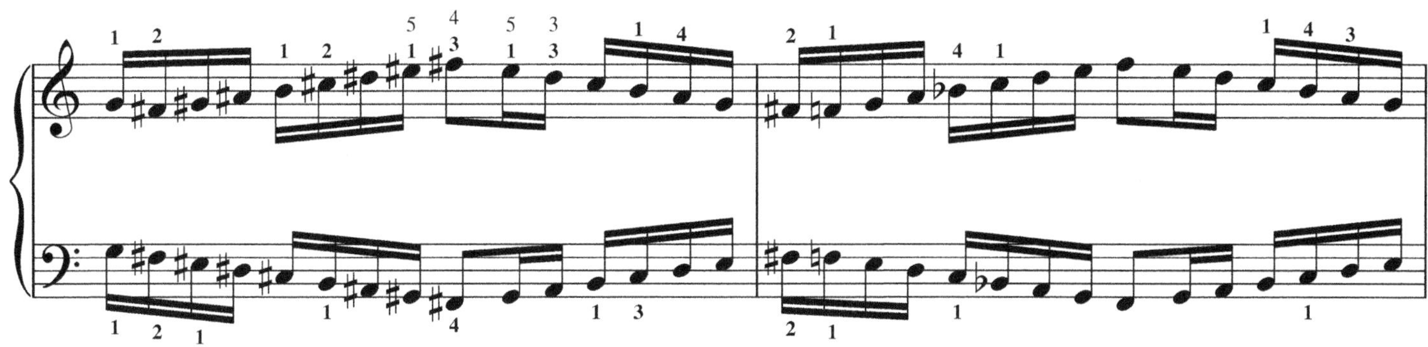

Same sequence in two octaves. Use the same fingering as in 5a for all connecting points between scales.

Work on finger flexibility. Experiment with crossing the longer fingers over the shorter ones.

6a

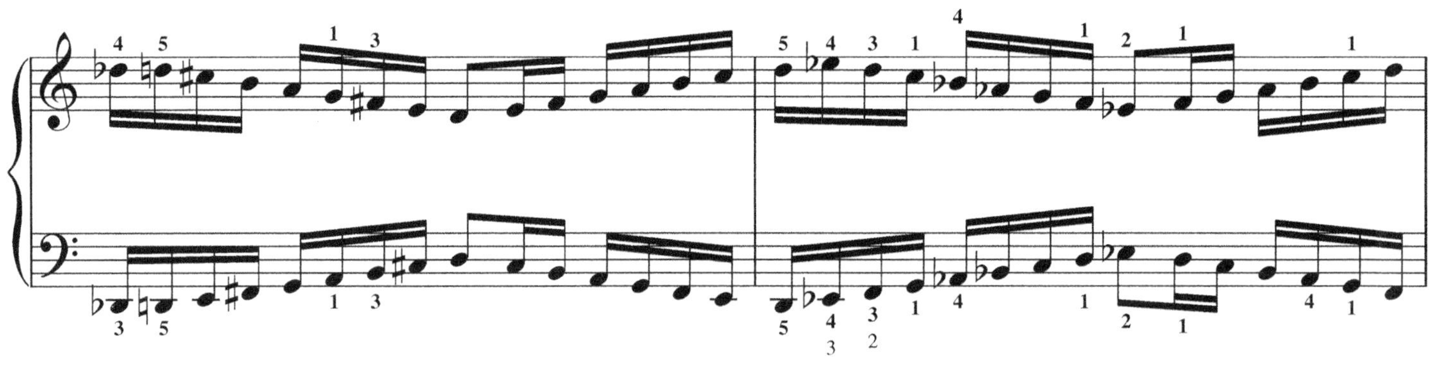

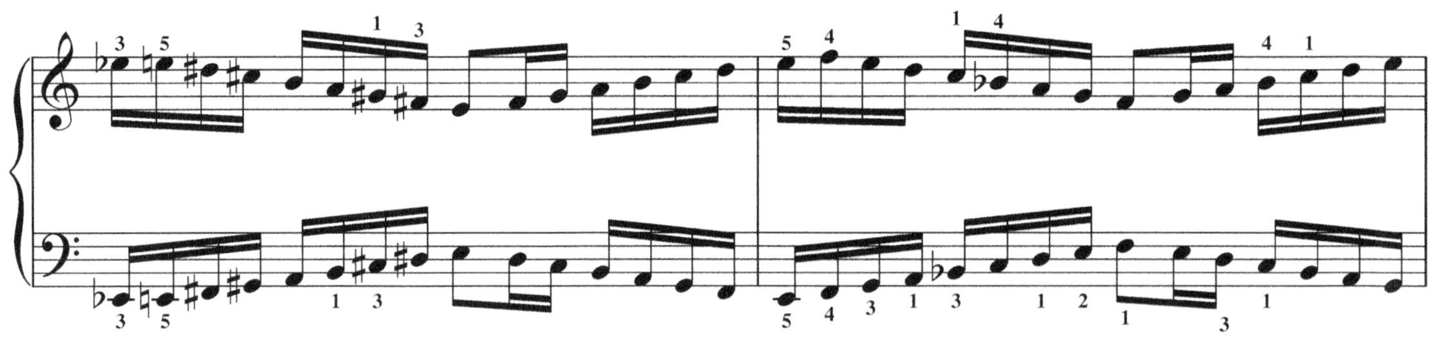

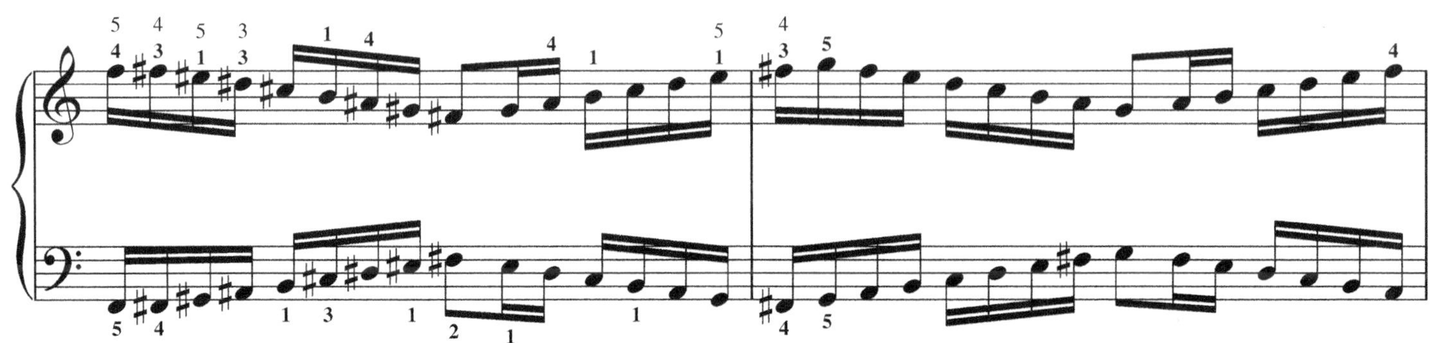

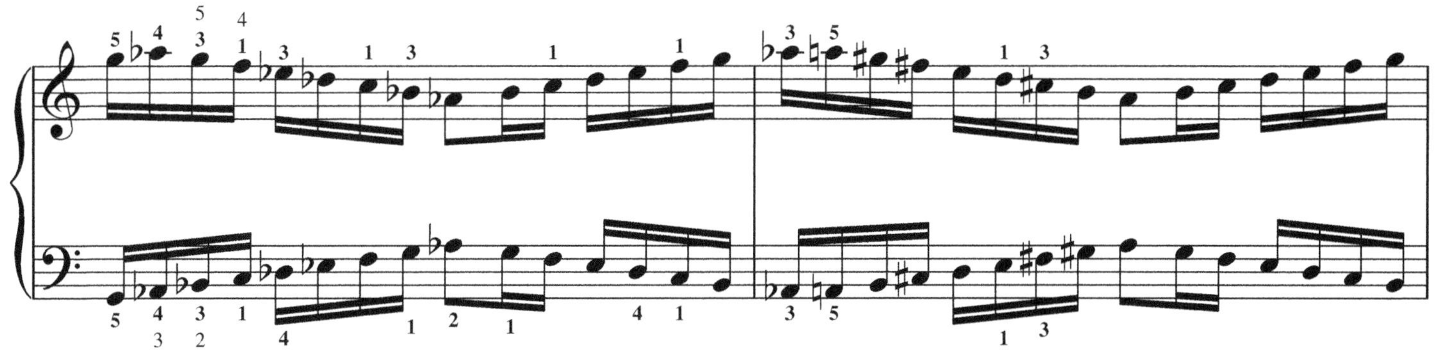

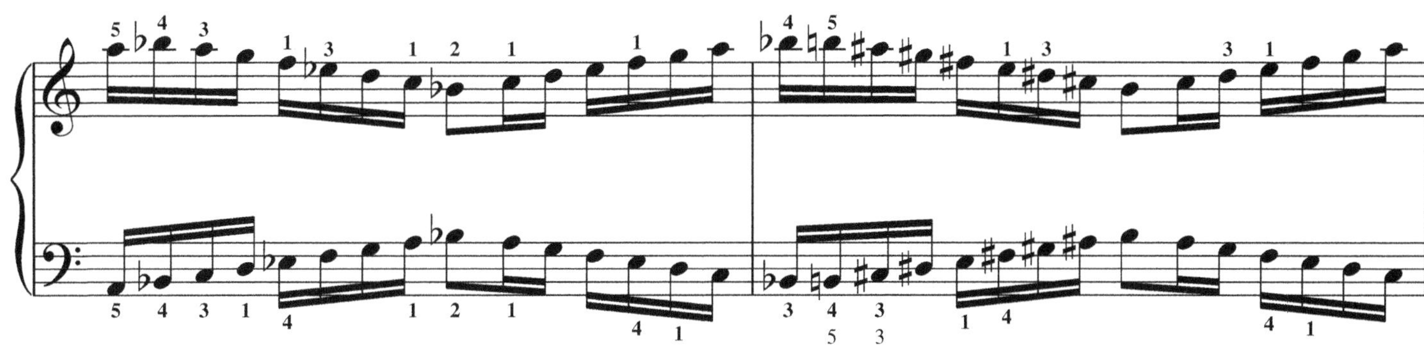

Same sequence in two octaves. Use the fingering of 6a in all connecting points between scales.

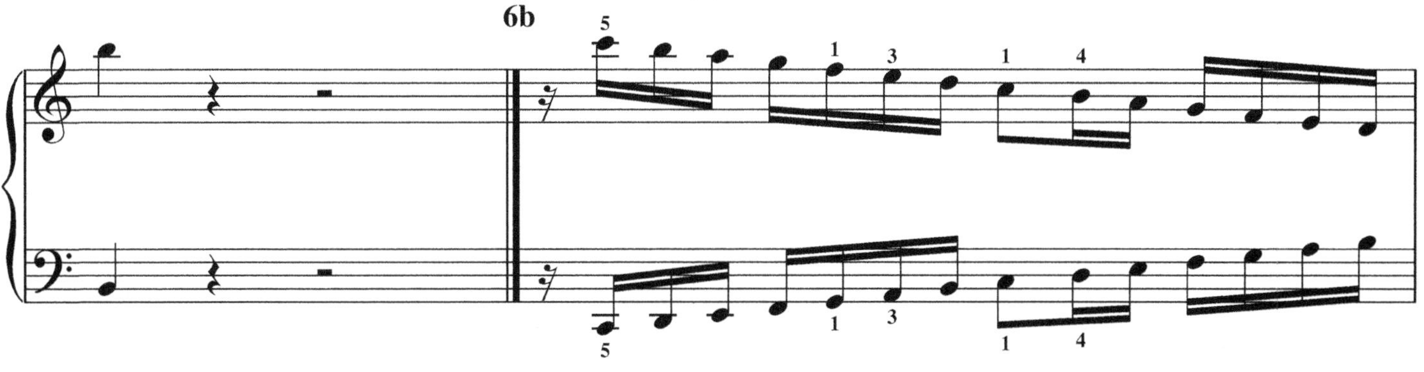

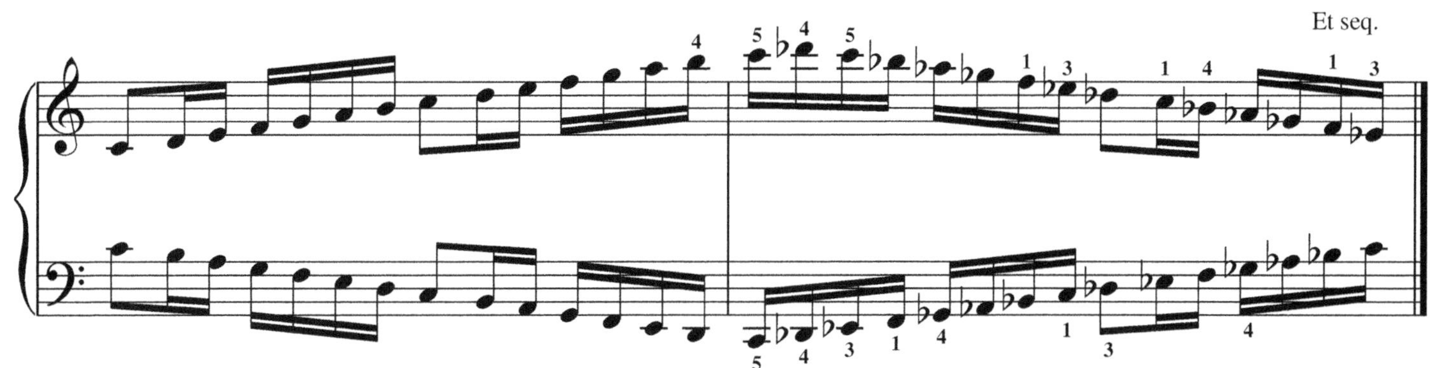

Parallel motion.

7a

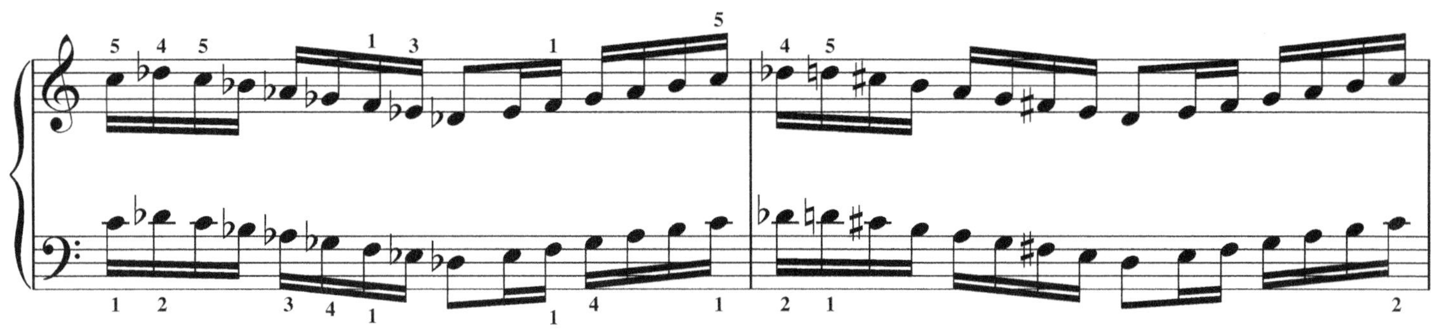

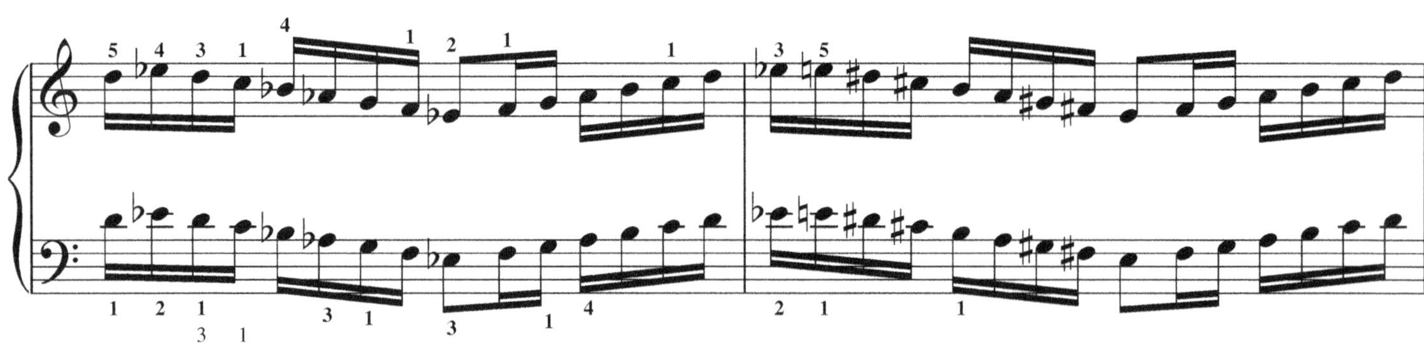

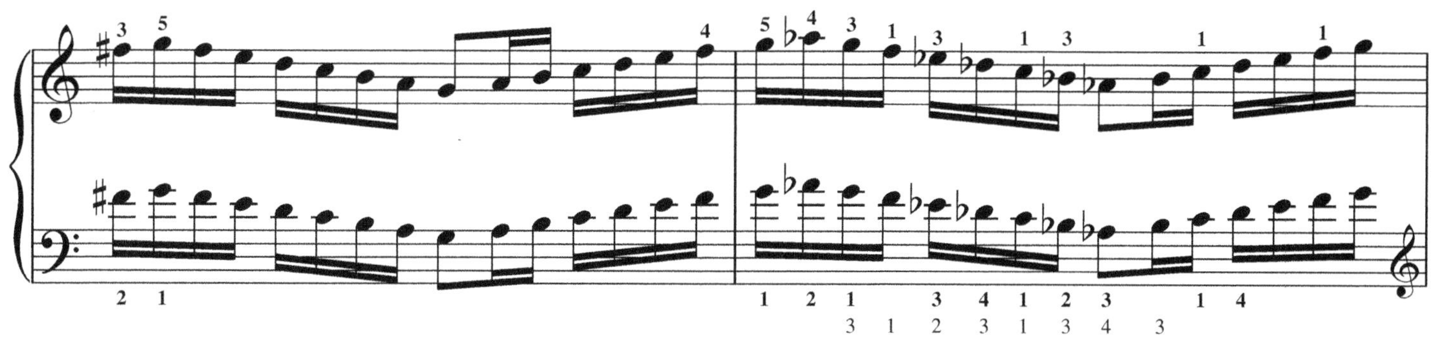

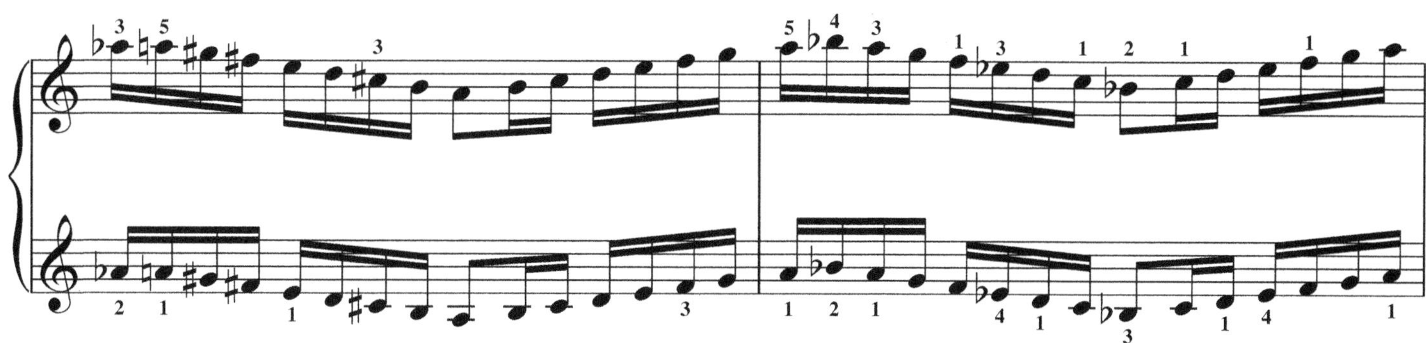

Same sequence in two octaves. Apply the fingering of 7a to connect all scales.

7b

Harmonic Minor.

8a

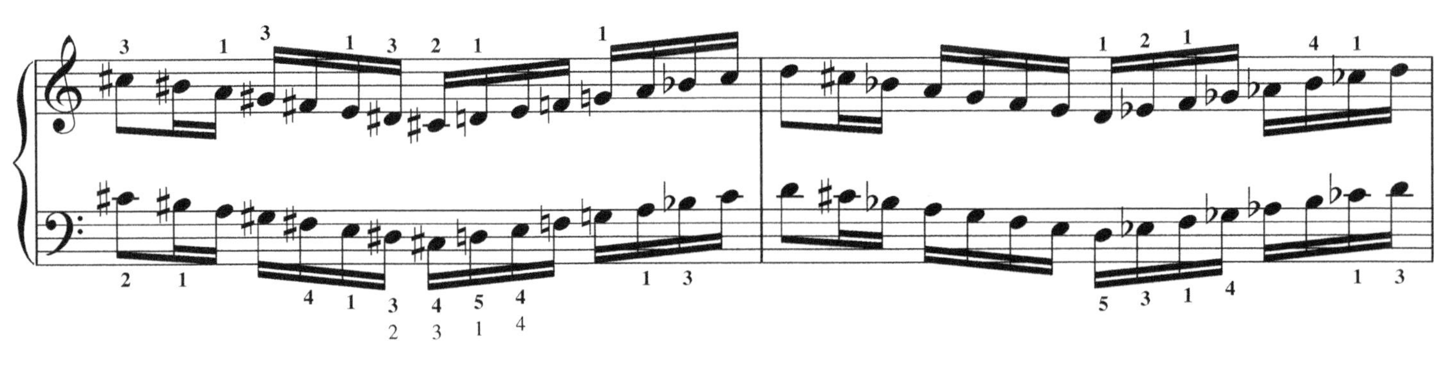

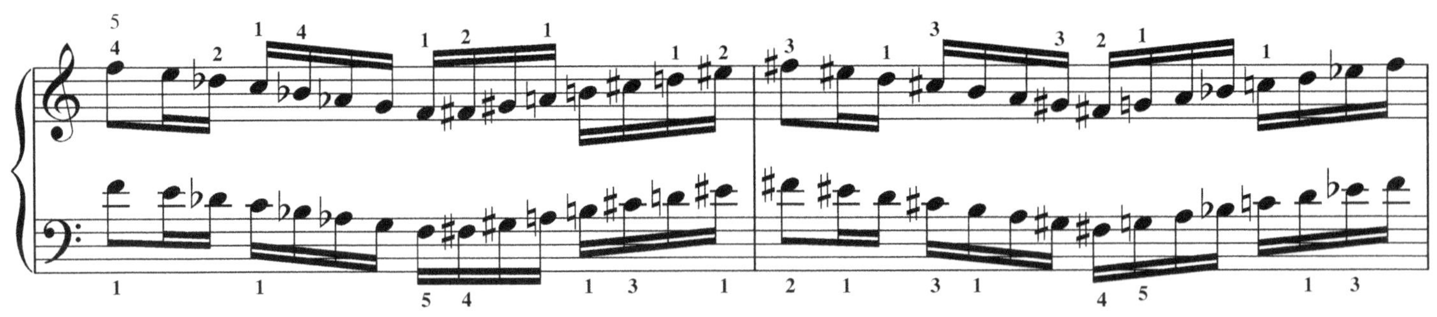

Same sequence in two octaves. Apply the fingering of 8a to connect all scales.

8b

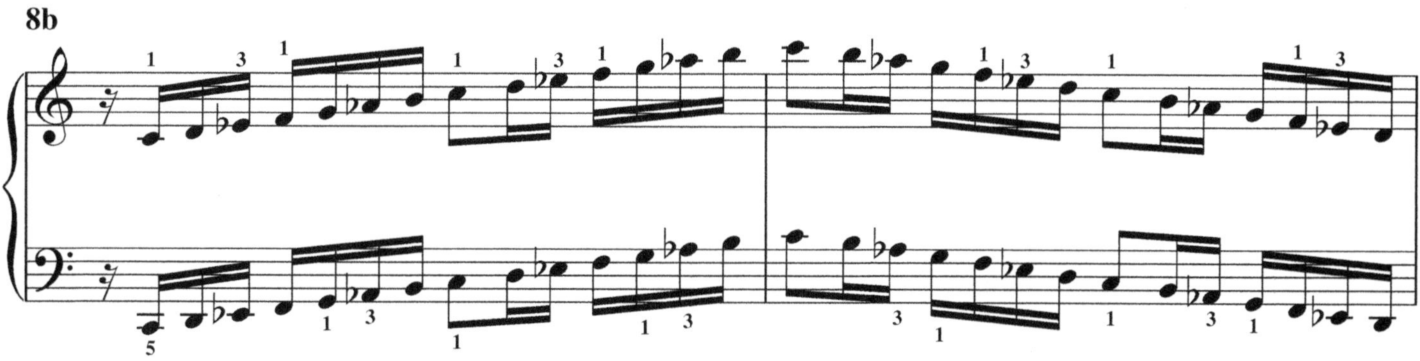

Et seq.

Melodic Minor.

9a

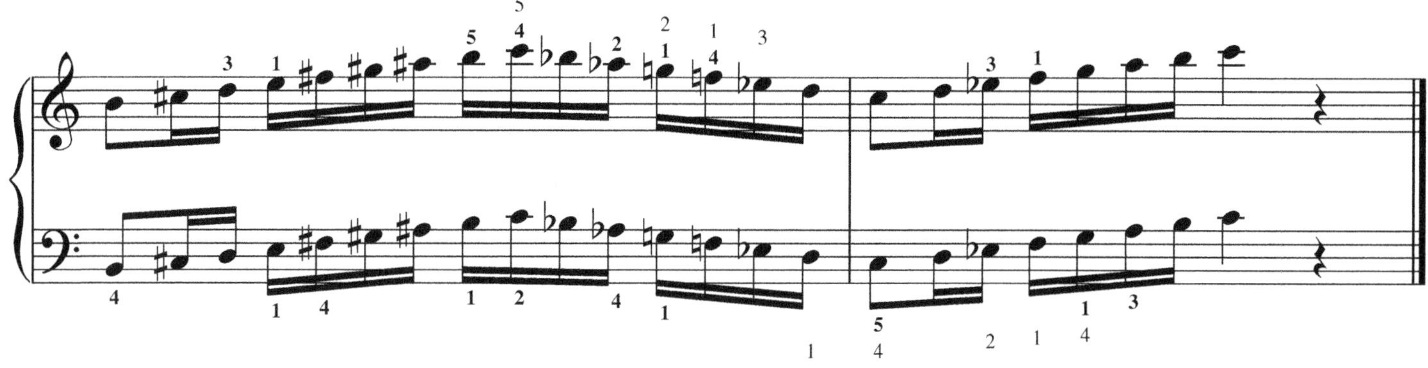

Same sequence in two octaves. Apply the fingering of 9a in all connecting points between scales.

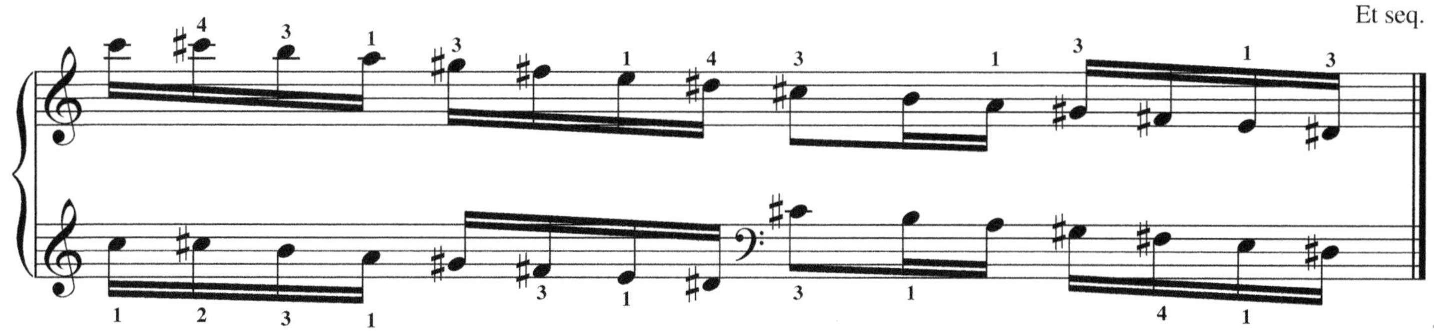

Chromatic scale preparation. You can begin all the chromatic scale warm-ups on any key.

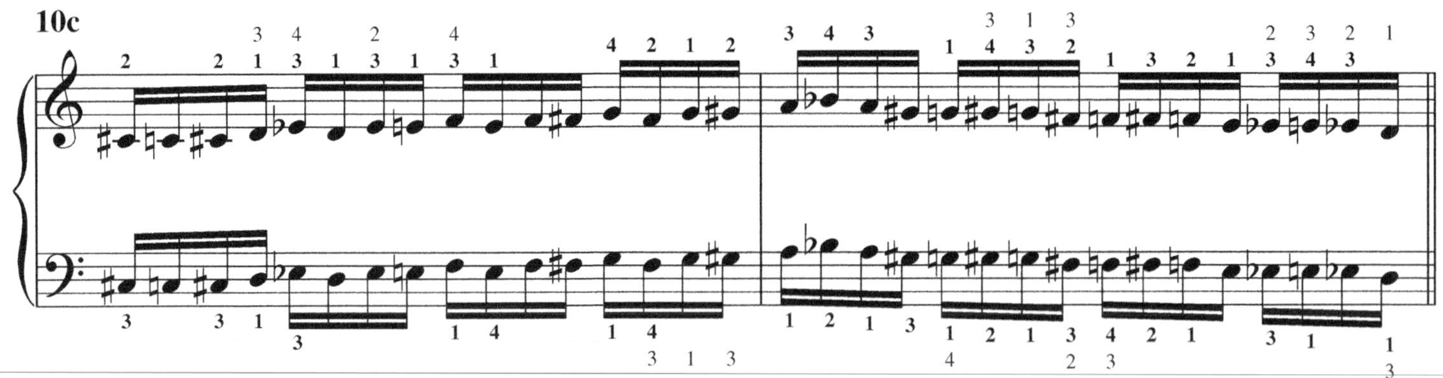

Chromatic scale.

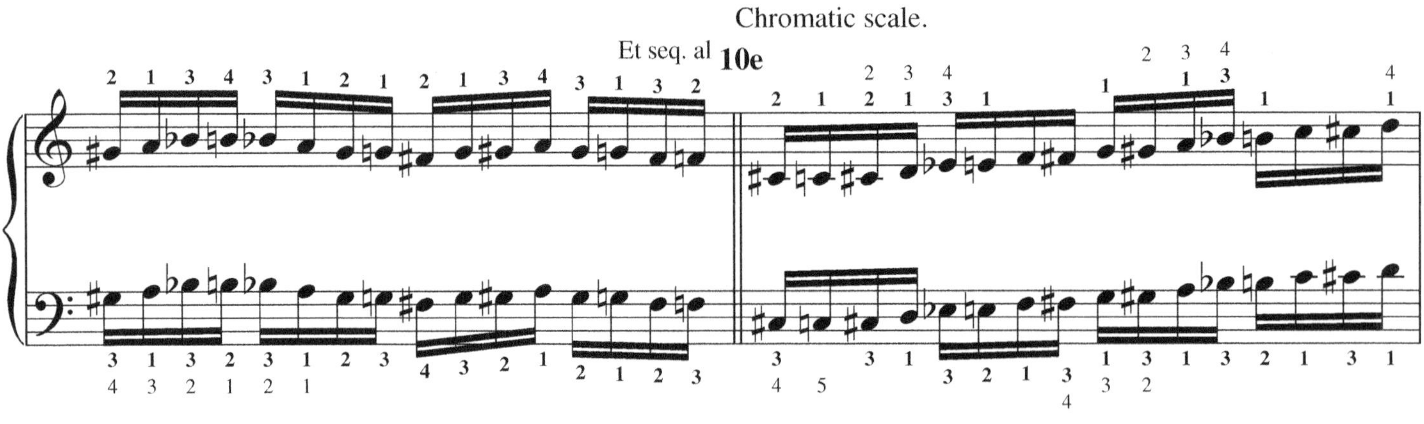

Chromatic patterns in triplets.

11a

11b

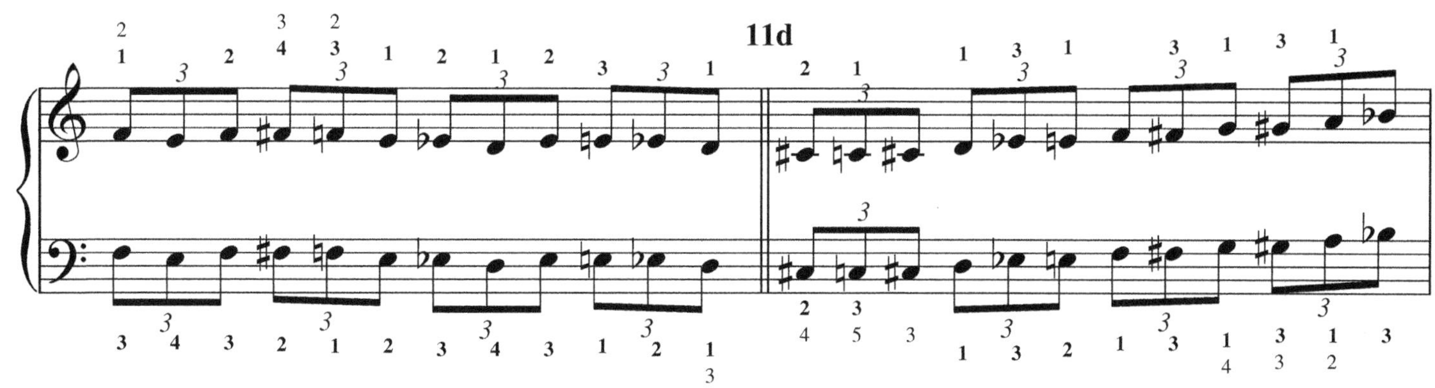

Section C–Arpeggiated figures and chord preparation

Feel the shft of the arm from the thumb to the fifth finger. Walk the hand back to the thumb.
Develop this most beneficial motion.
1a
1b
1c
1d
1e

1f
1g
1h
1i
Et seq.
1k
1l
Et seq.
Practice both legato and staccato.
Play 2a–2e in a row, then reverse the order and play up one half step. Keep chaining up in this zig-zag, ascending-descending order.
1m
Et seq.
2a
2b
2c
8va
3a
3b

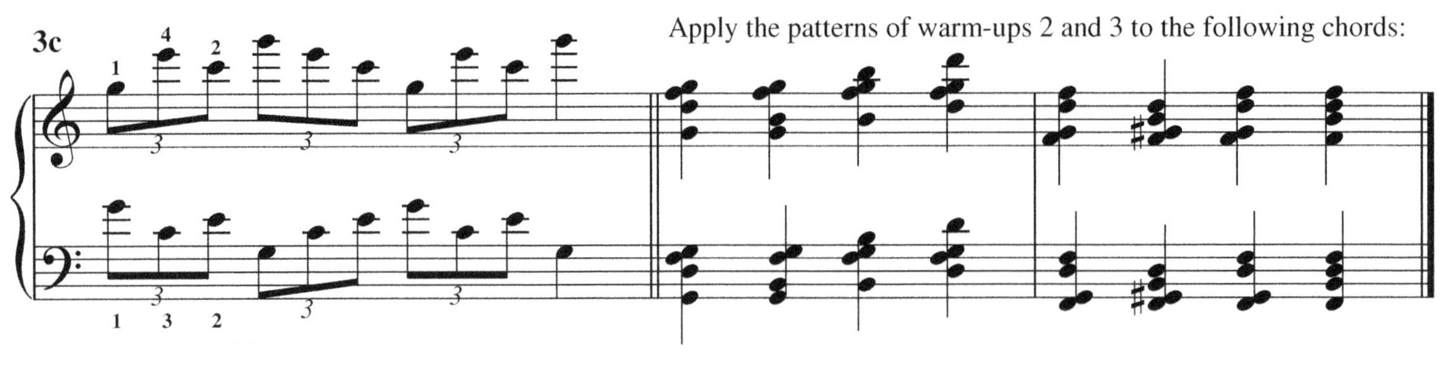
3c
Apply the patterns of warm-ups 2 and 3 to the following chords:

4a

4b

4c

4d

5a
Continue applying the same motives to the following chords:
(The diminished seventh chord will be played as follows.)
5b
(You can substitute the ascending part of the previous exercise with the following variation).
Et seq.

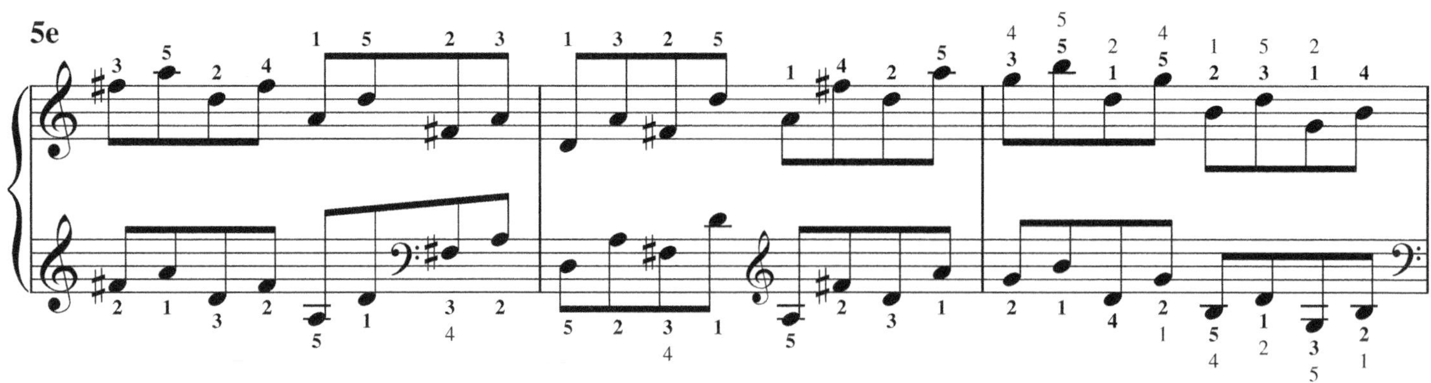
5e

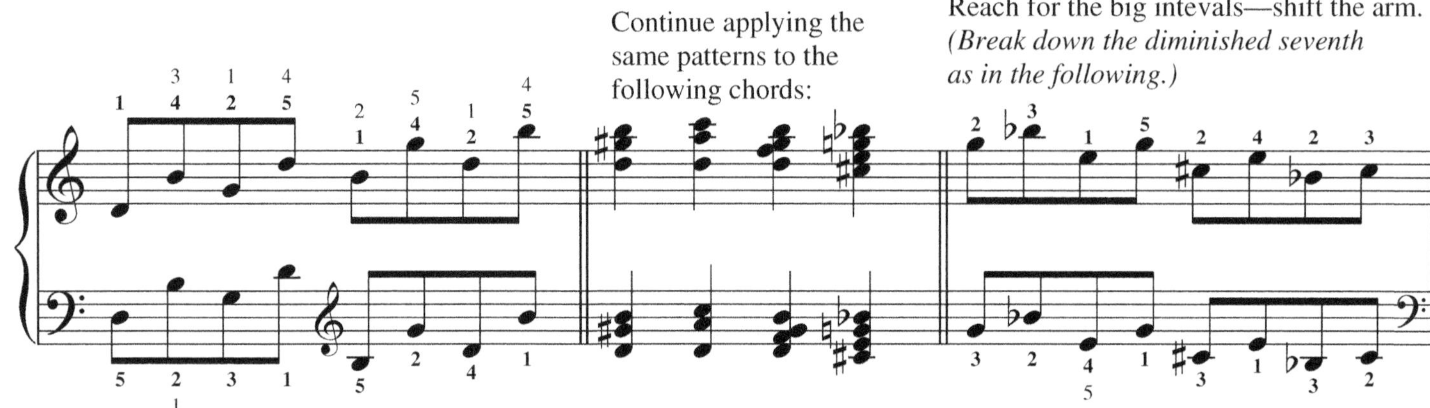
Continue applying the same patterns to the following chords:
Reach for the big intevals—shift the arm.
(Break down the diminished seventh as in the following.)

(Substitute the previous measure with the following variation.)

In 6a–6c apply the same order and trasposition technique as in 2a–2c.

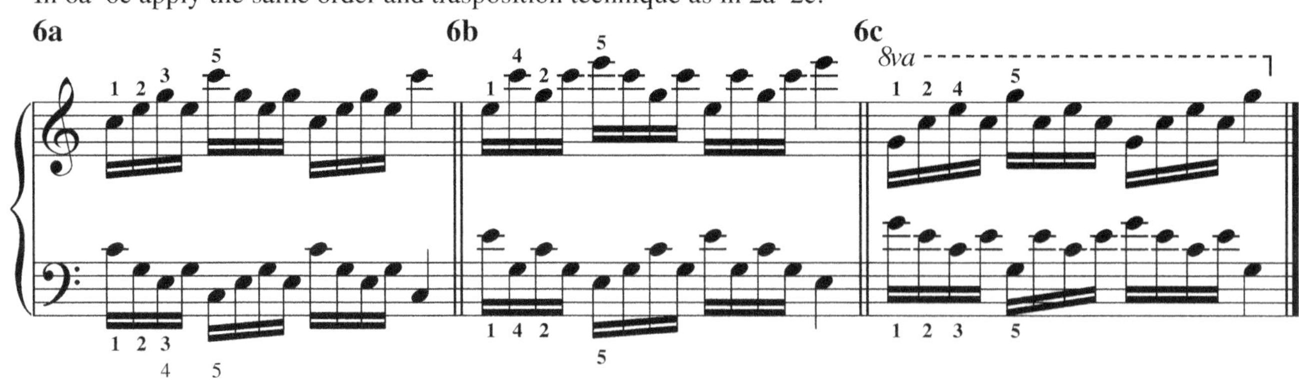
6a
6b
6c
8va

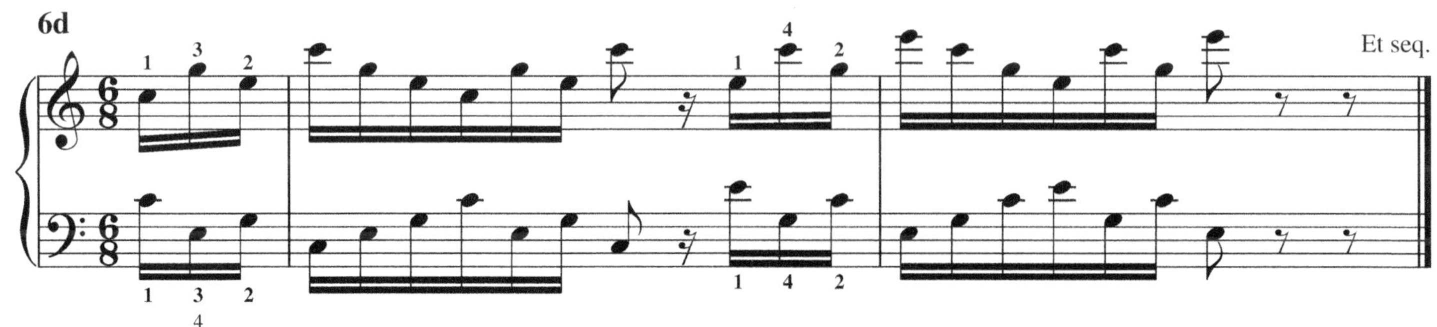
6d
Et seq.

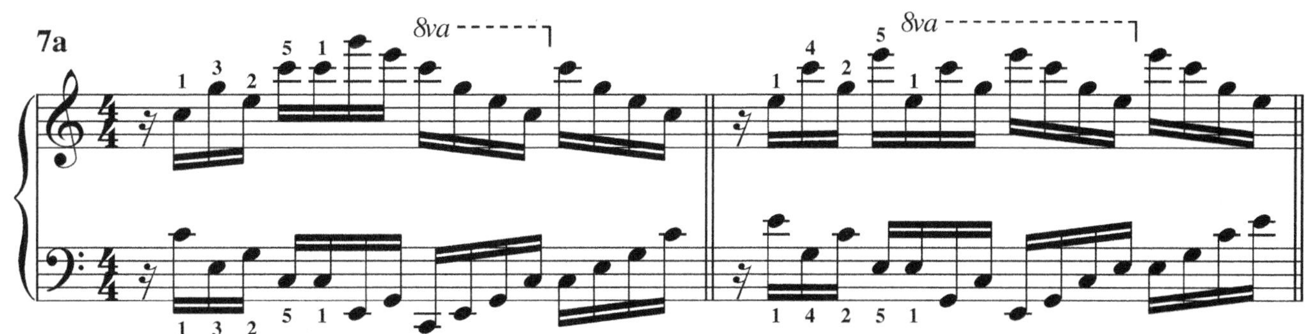

7b

8va

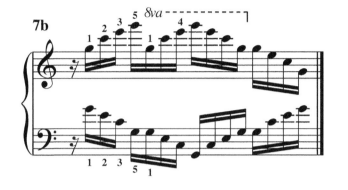

Dominant seventh chords.
Develop the stretches between the fingers
in a mild dynamic and tempo.

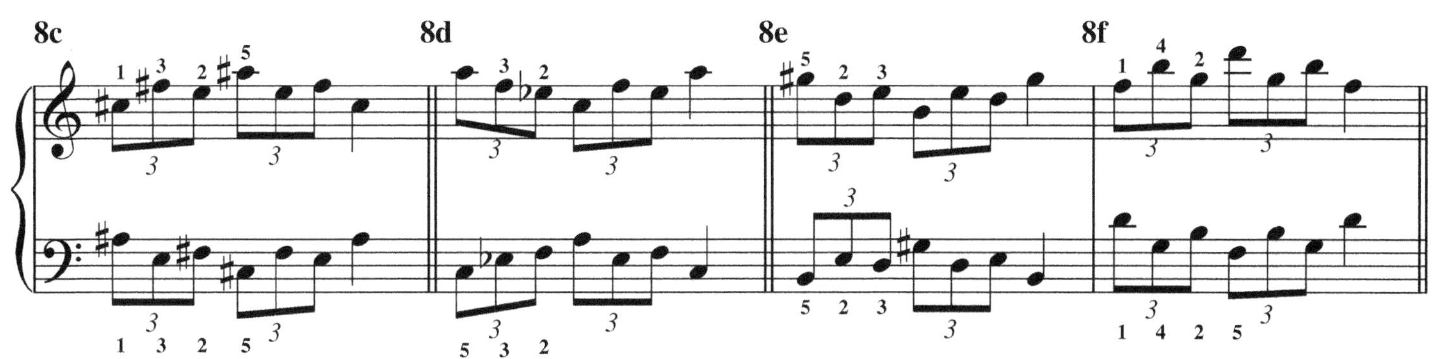

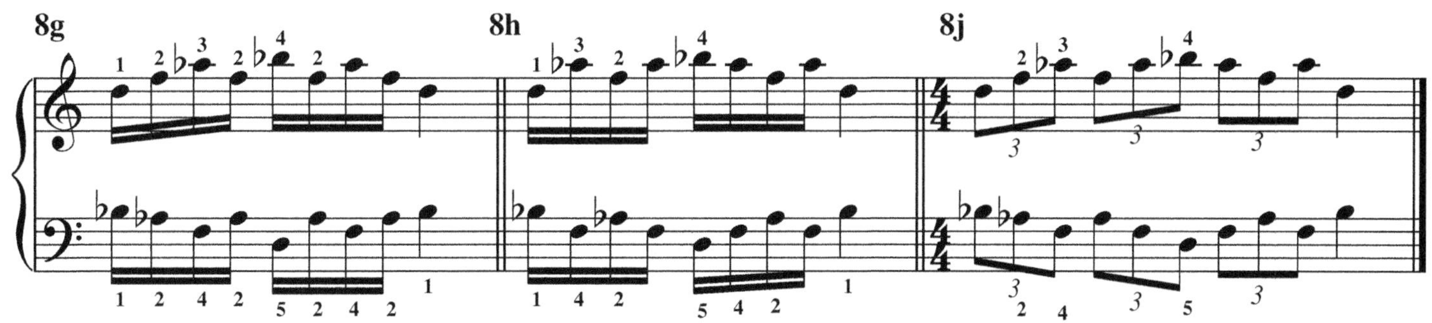

Feel a powerful arm pull toward the chord.

More advanced students can alternate selected patterns from 8 and 9 with exercises 15–17.

Apply the motives from exercises 8 and 9 to the following chords:

Maintain a gentle, undulating arm motion throughout.

Et seq.

Substitute the ascending part of the previous exercise with the following: *(given here in D Major for sample fingerings in a sharp key.)*

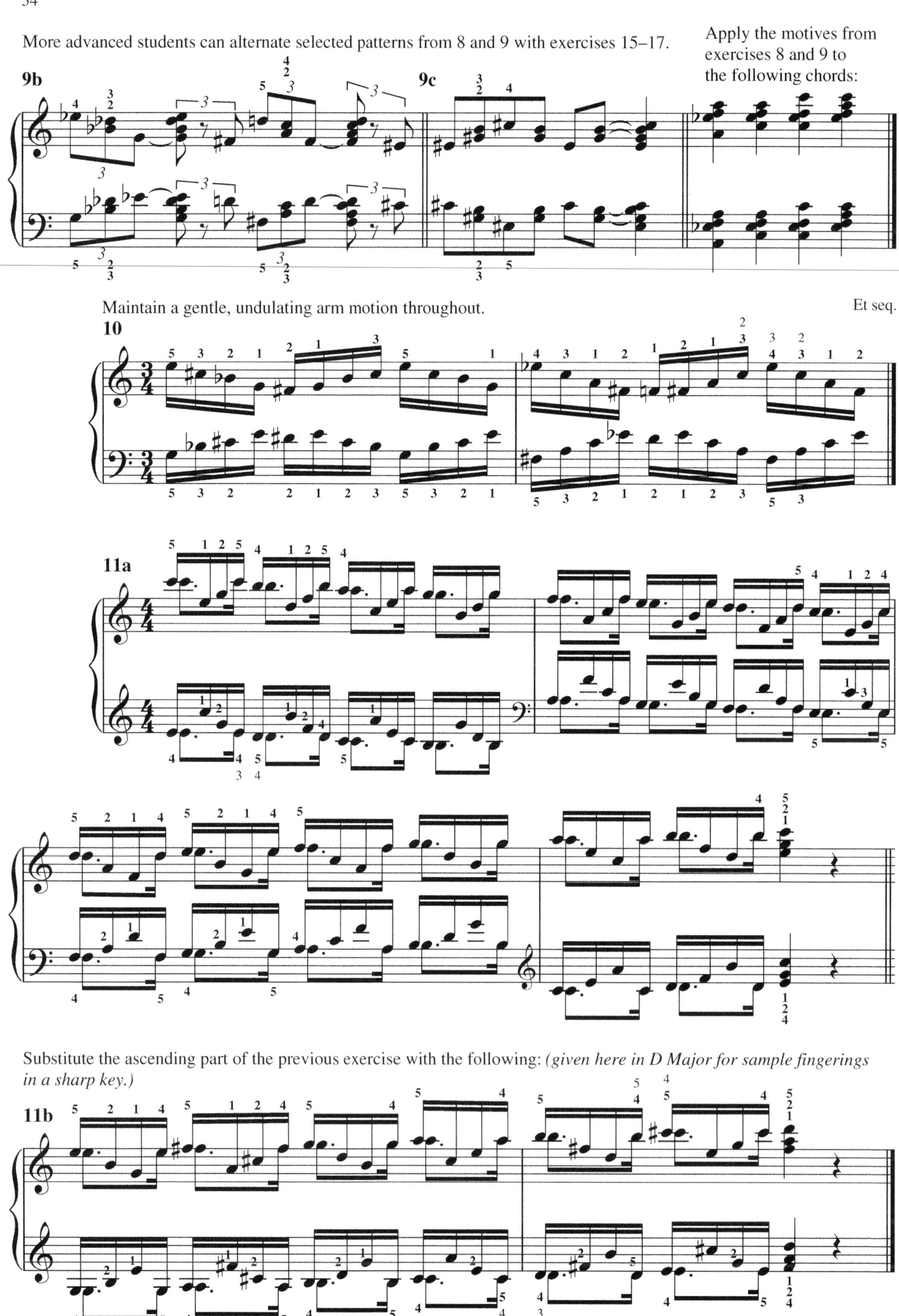

Point of support in fingers 4-5.

Diminished chord preparation.

Diminished and dominant seventh chords combined.

Full chord preparation (interval of the octave).

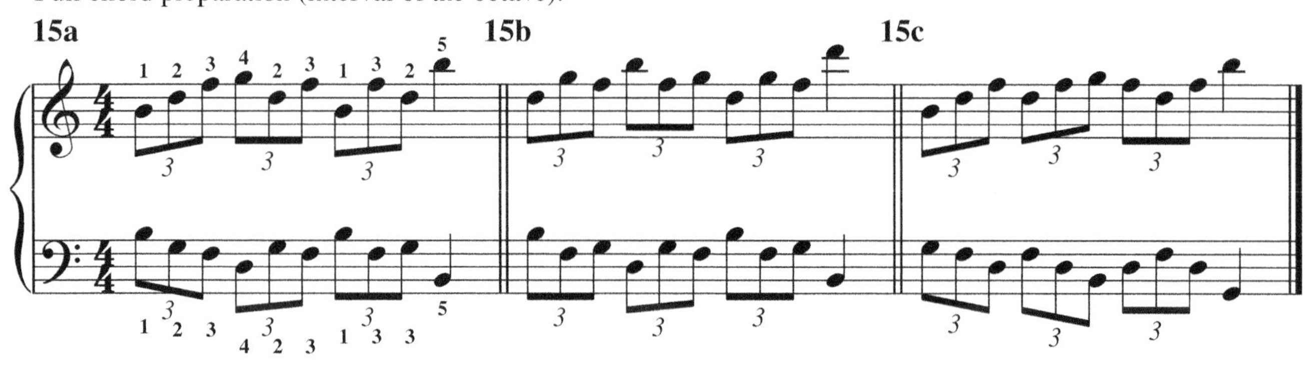

Apply the same motive in the following chords:

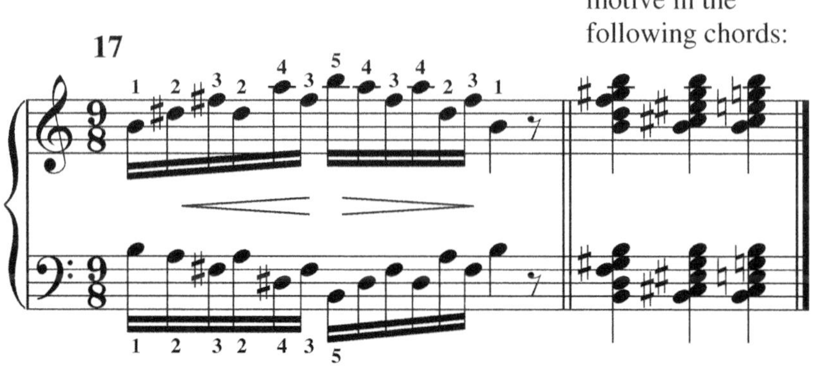

You can practice 18a-20c in a continuous way by omitting the notes and rests within the brackets.

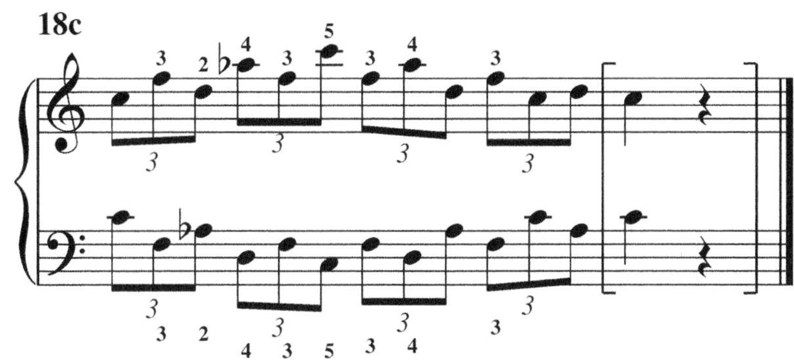

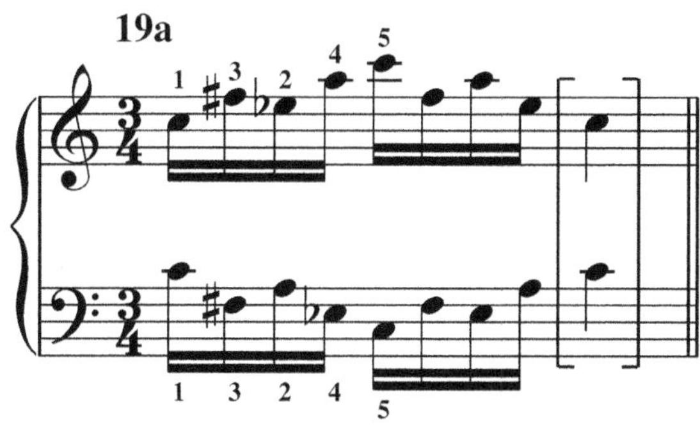

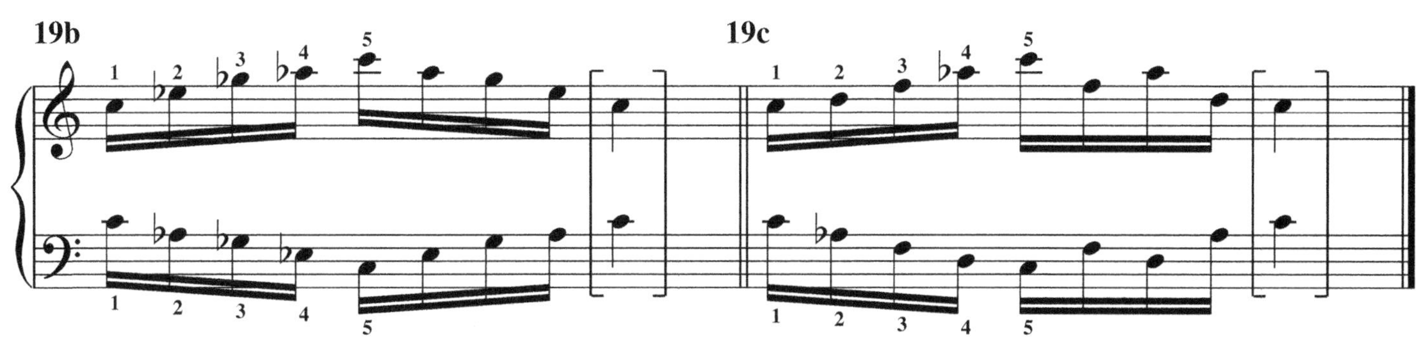

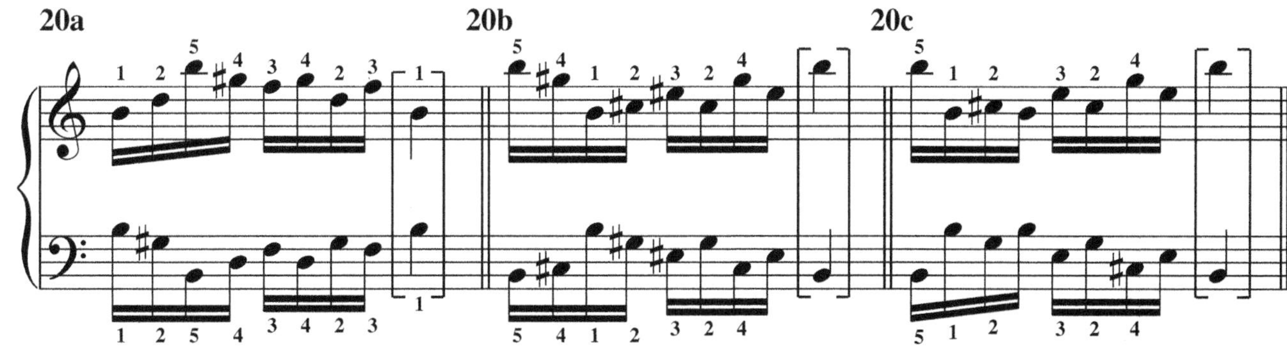

Diminished, dominant and half diminished seventh chords combined. Finger stretch development. Begin in a mild tempo and dynamic.

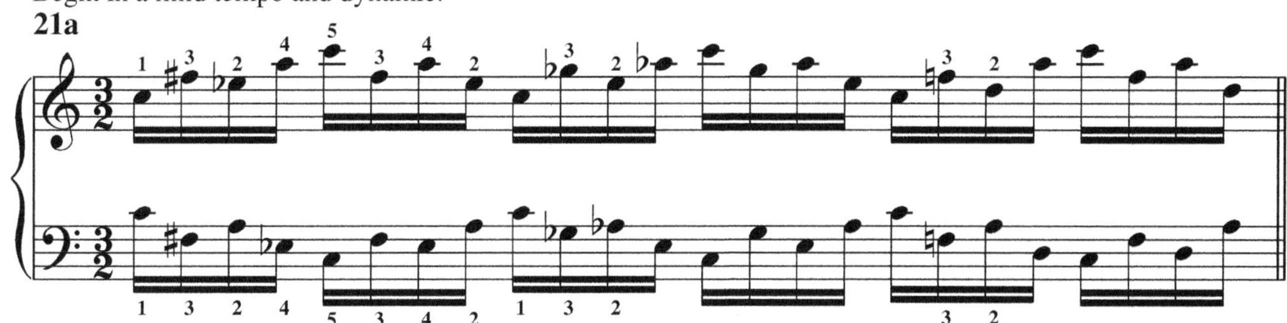

21b

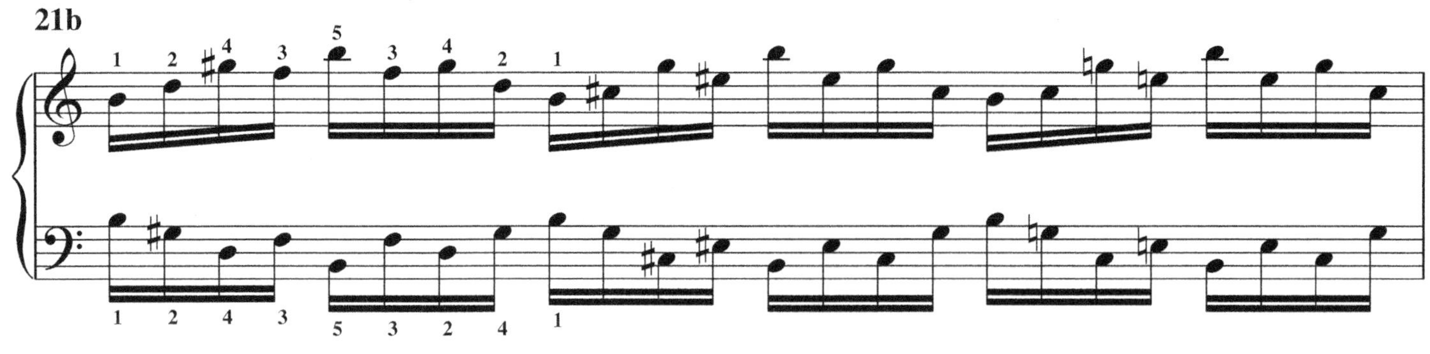

21c

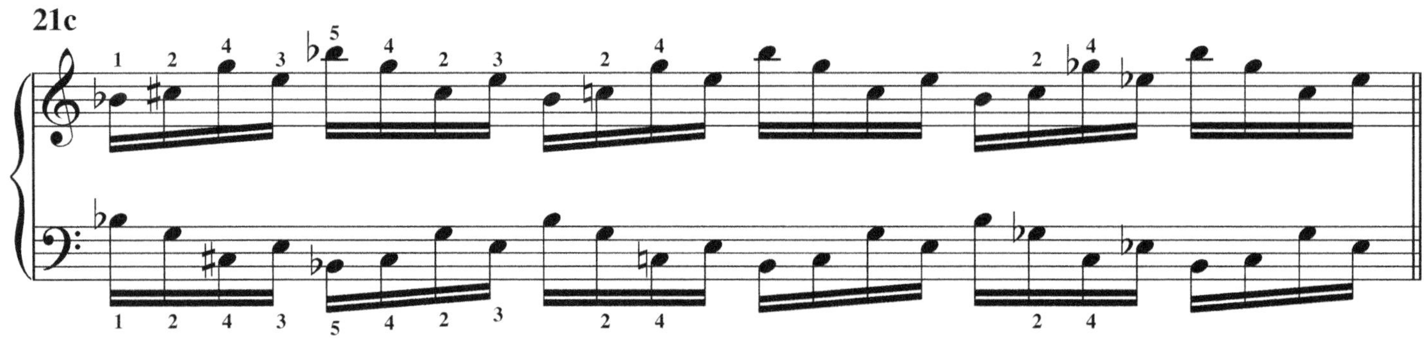

21d

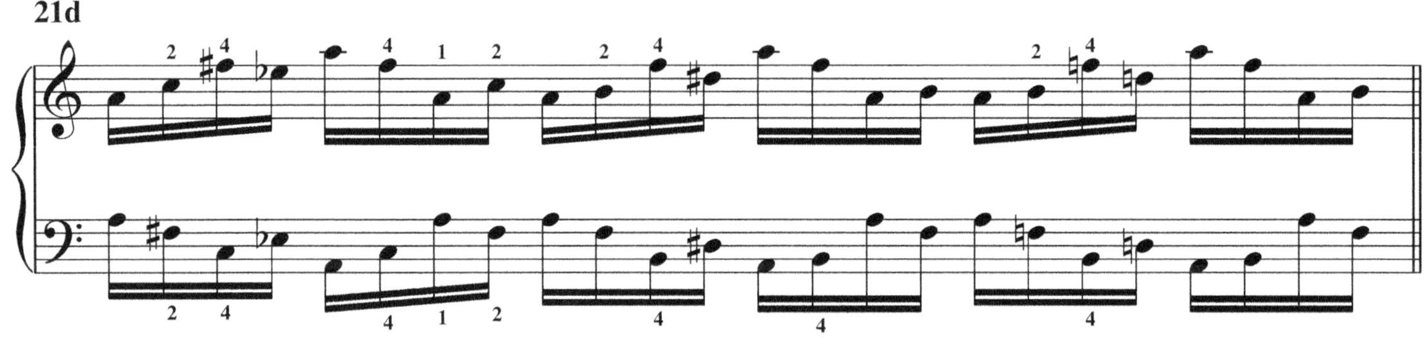

21e

21f

Et seq.

Arpeggio sequences in one and two octaves.

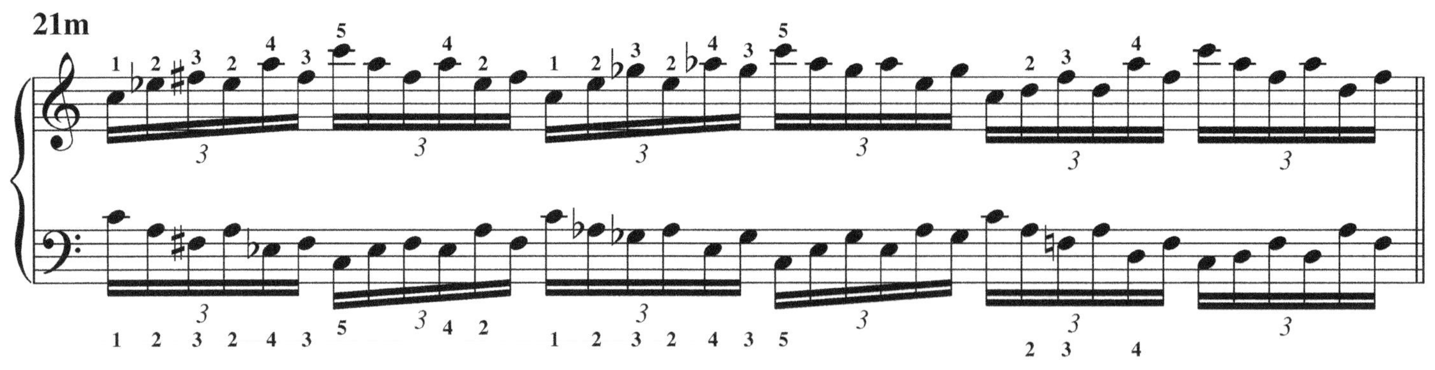

21n

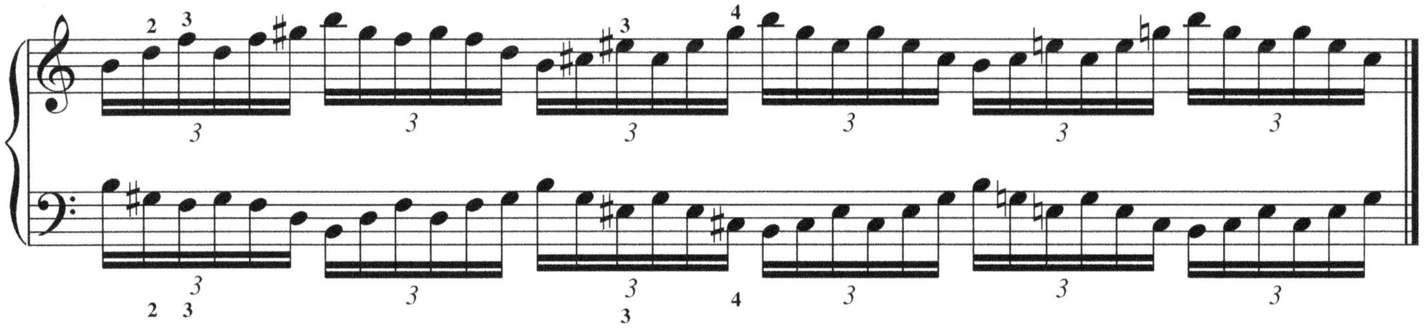

22a

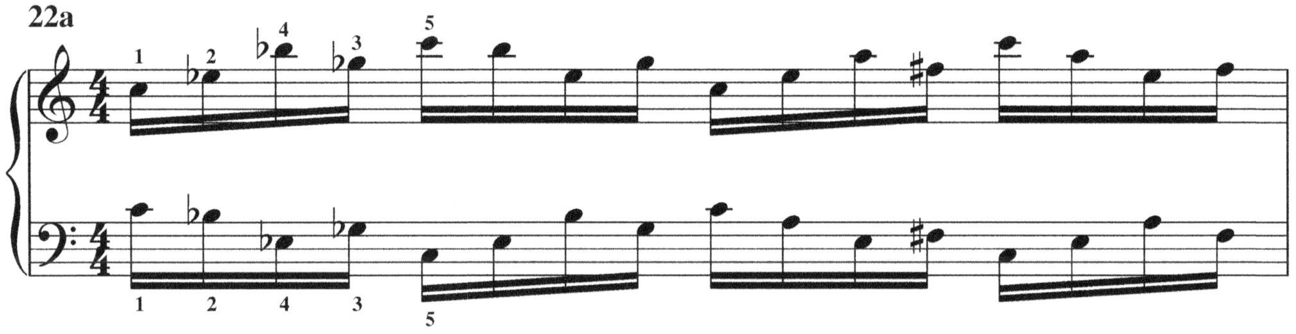

22b

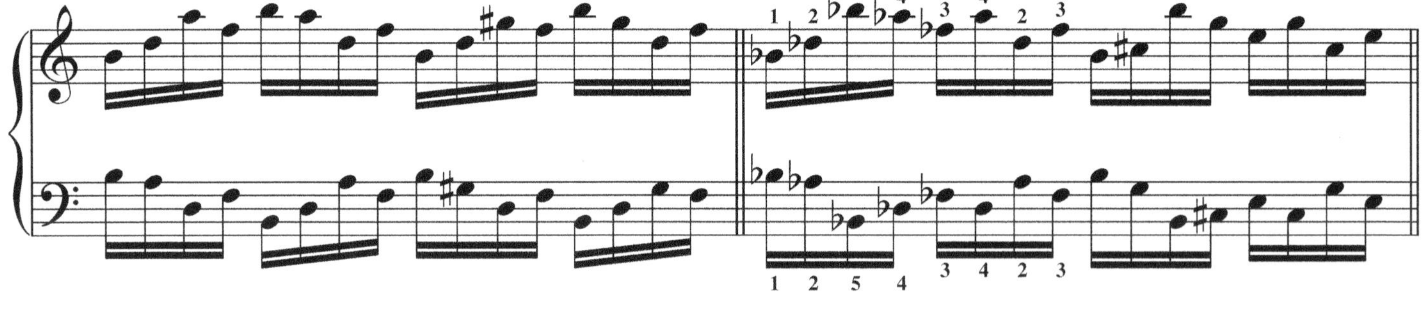

22c

22d

Et seq.

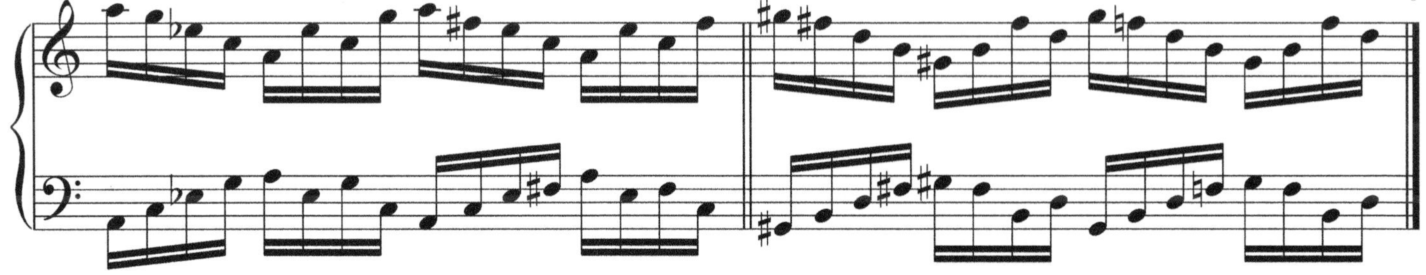

As soon as you reach the 5th finger, swing the arm back to the thumb.

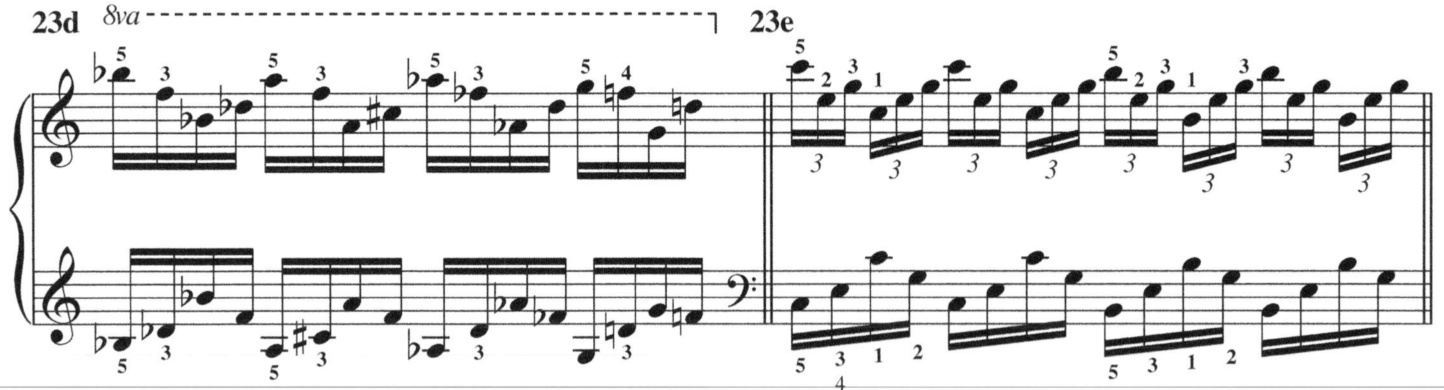
23d
8va
23e

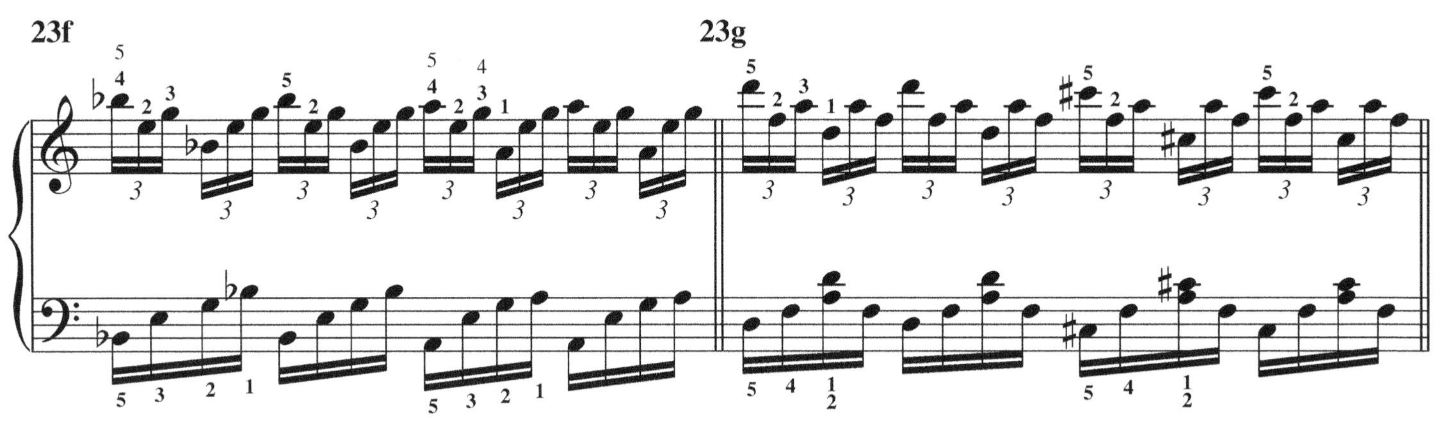
23f
23g

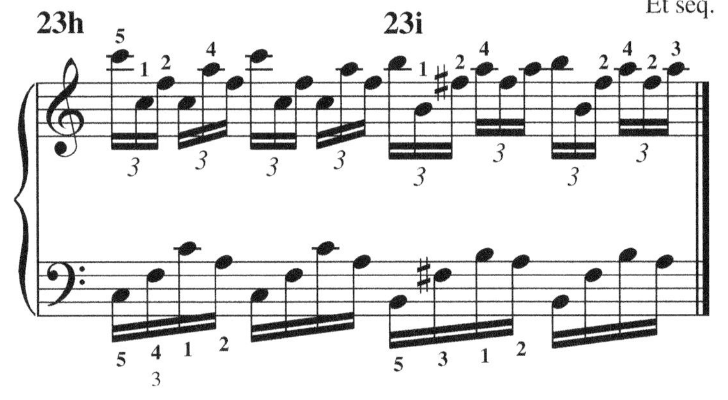
23h
23i
Et seq.

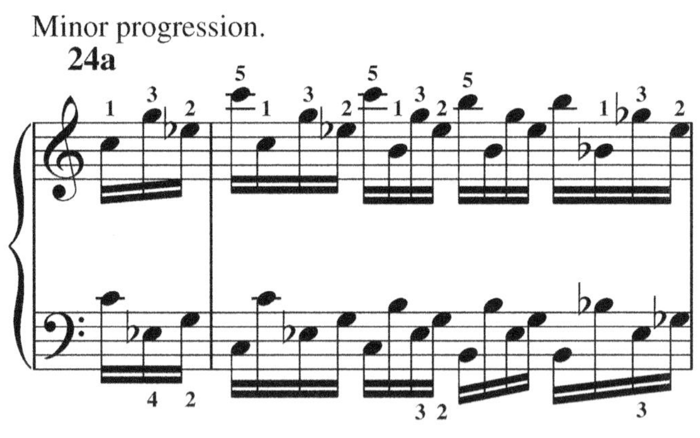
Minor progression.
24a

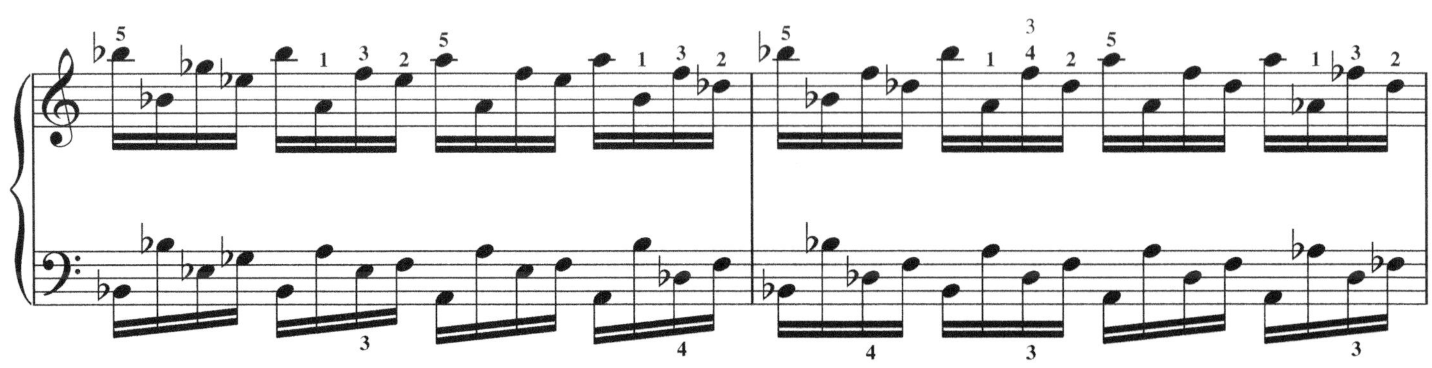

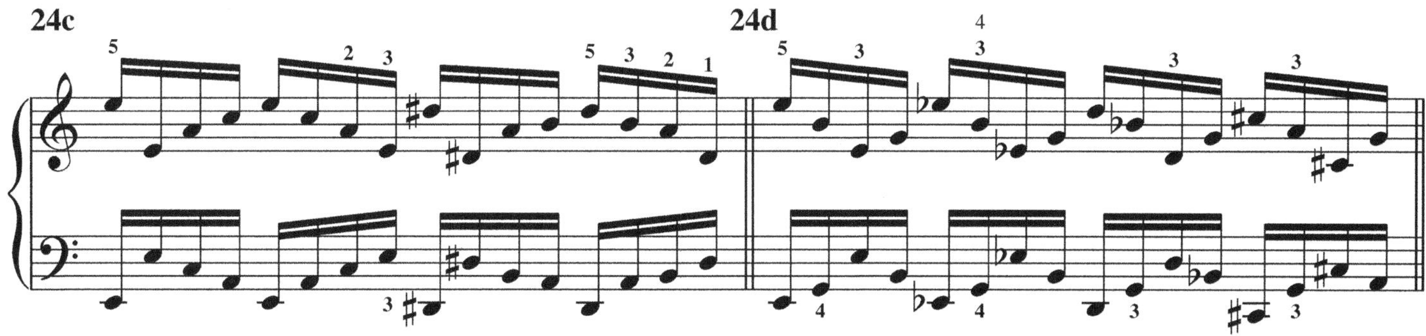

Observe the symmetry of the two hands, facing in opposite directions.

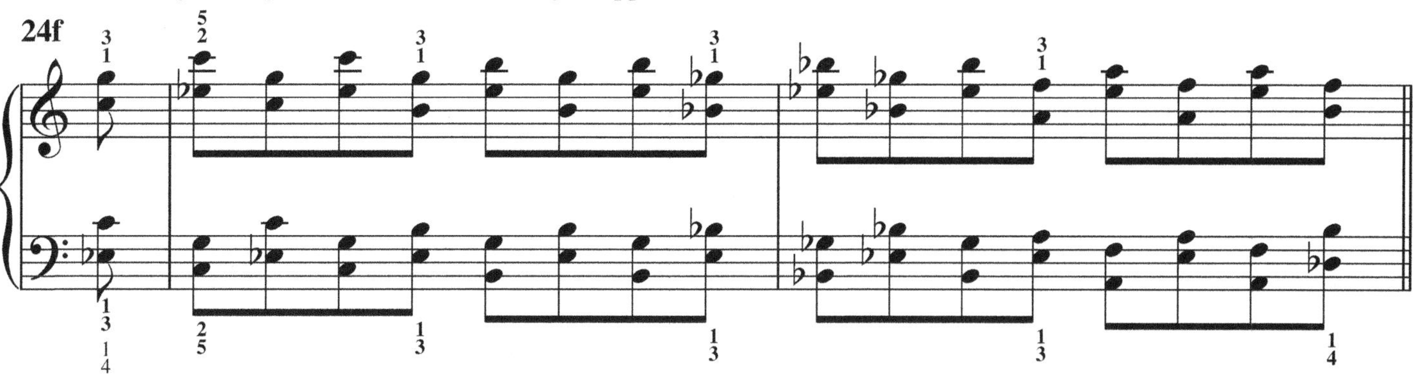

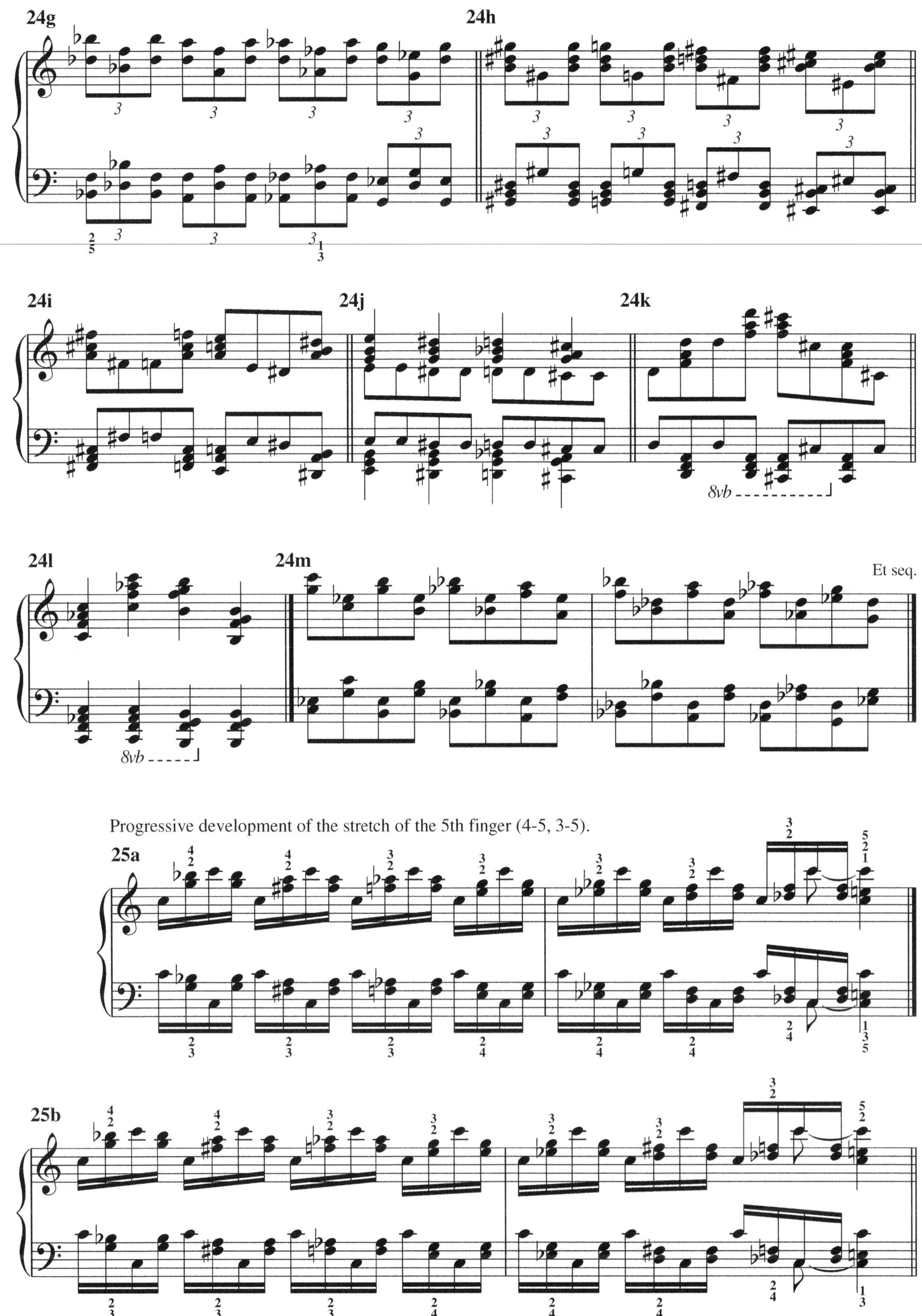
24g
24h
24i
24j
24k
8vb
24l
8vb
24m
Et seq.
Progressive development of the stretch of the 5th finger (4-5, 3-5).
25a
25b

(Follow the same chord sequence as in 25.)
26a
Et seq.
26b
Et seq.
26c
Et seq.
26d
Et seq.
26e
Et seq.
26f
Et seq.
26g
8va
8va
Et seq. al
End up as follows:
8va

Release the thumb when playing each chord (as in the previous exercises).

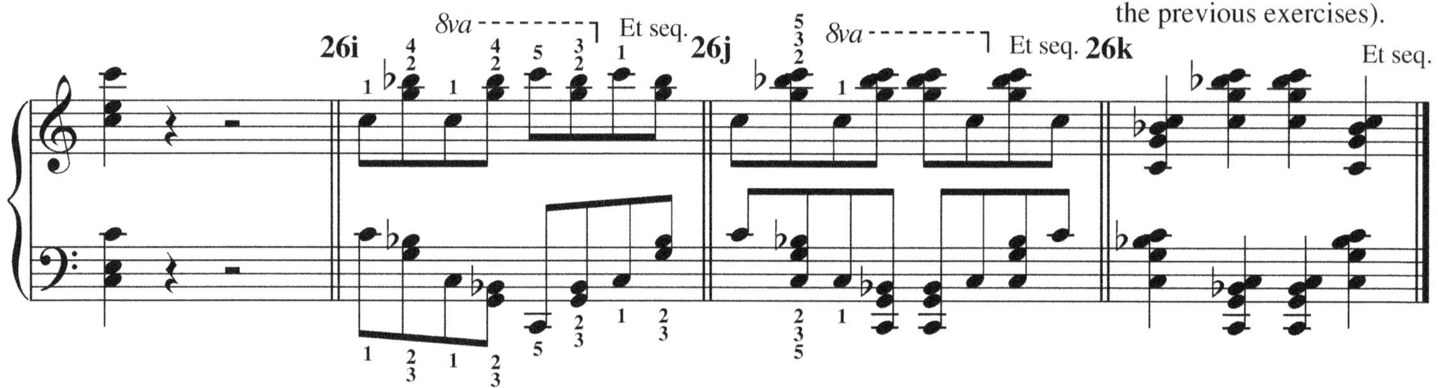

Dominant, half-diminished, and fully-diminished seventh chord arpeggiated figures.

Et seq.
Added sixth chord.
28a
(Also try 28d with an F natural-minor added sixth.)
28b
28c
28d
(Practice 28e in minor as well.)
28e
Et seq.
29a

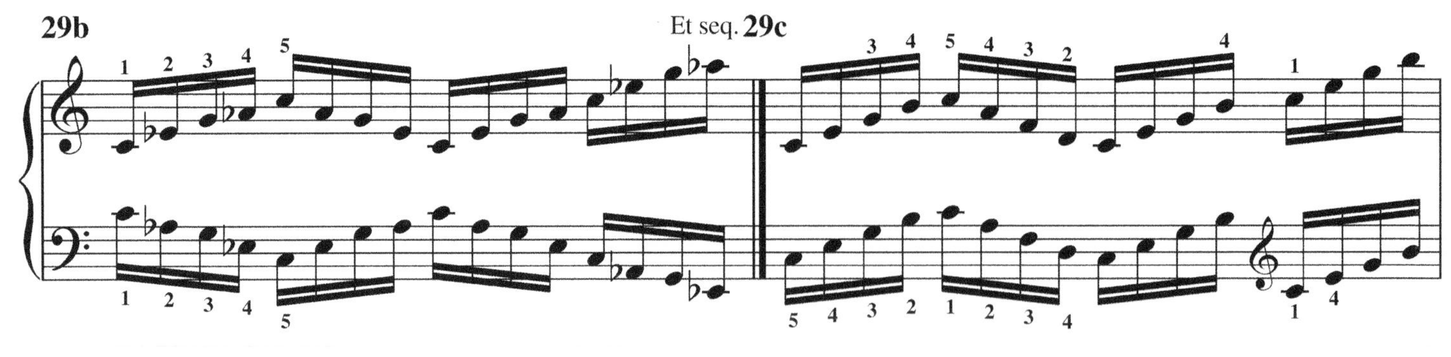

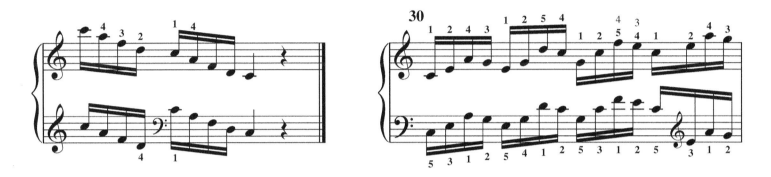

Extended dominant seventh arpeggiated figures. Feel the arm "walking" through the fingers.

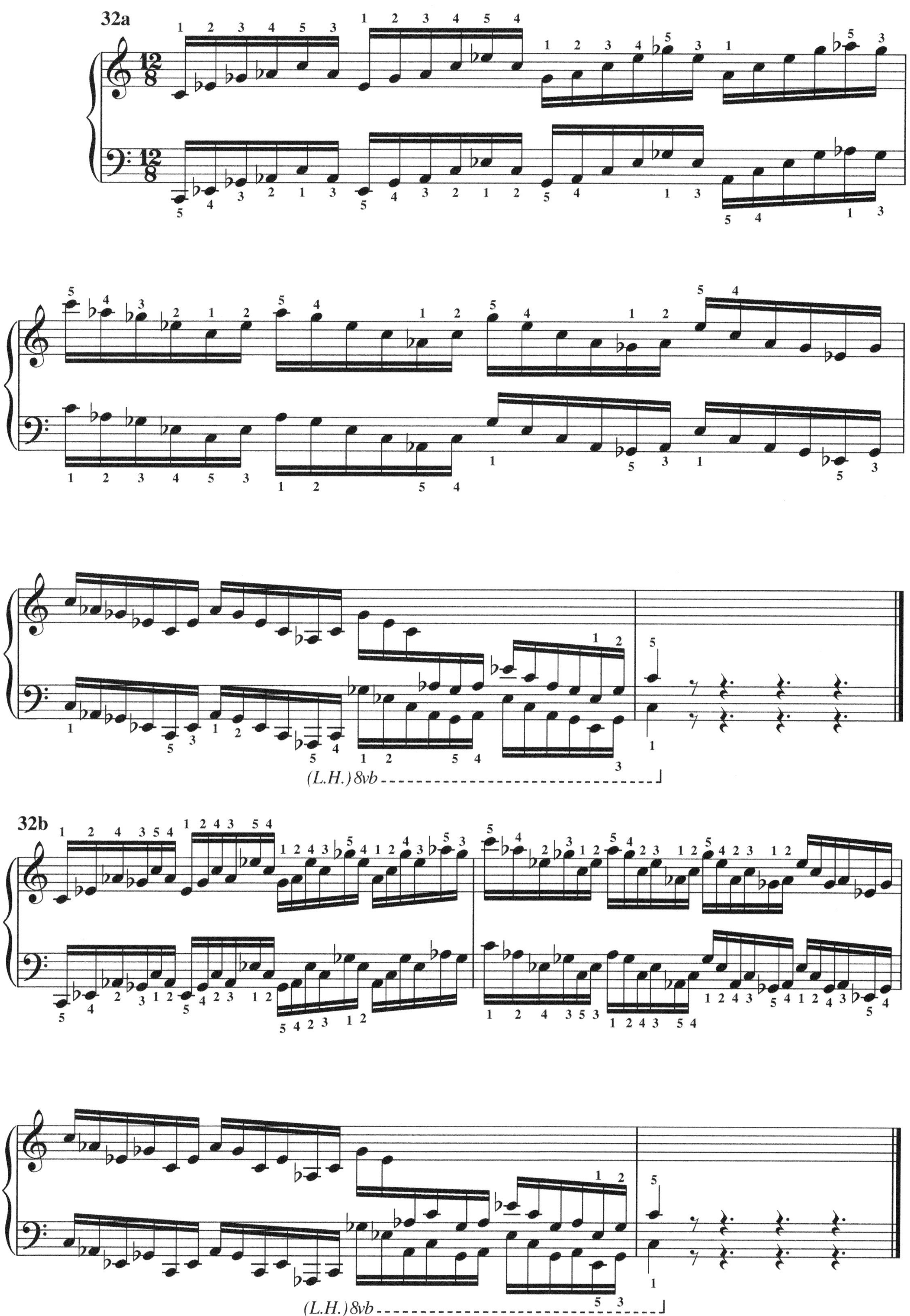
32a
(L.H.) 8vb
32b
(L.H.) 8vb

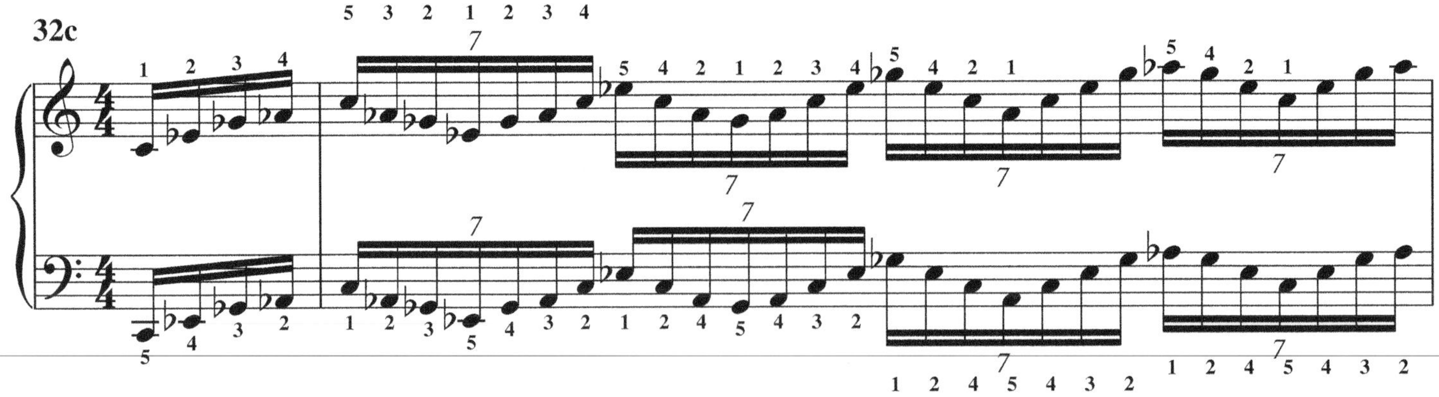

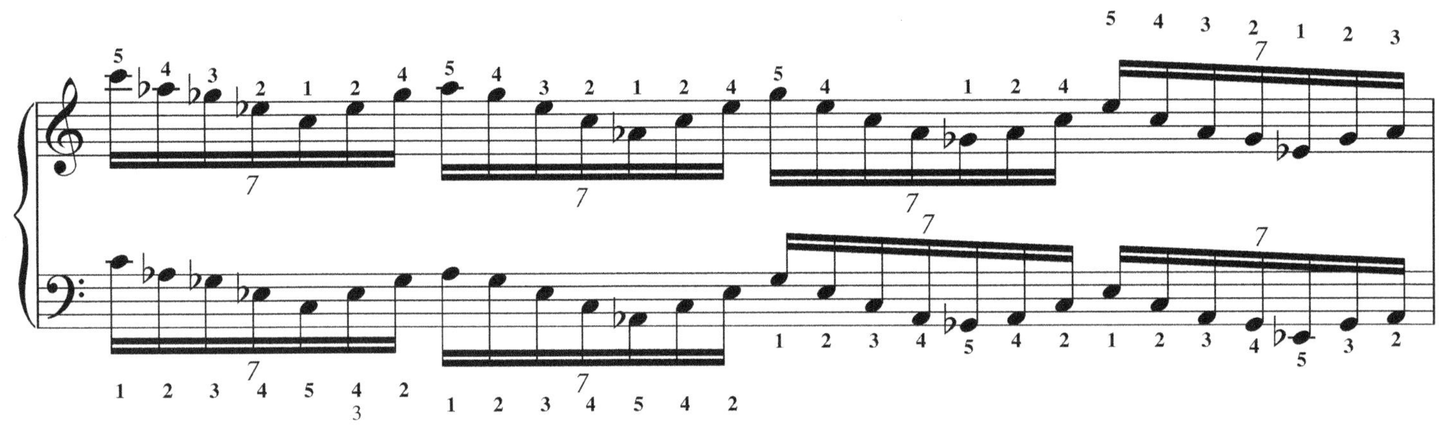

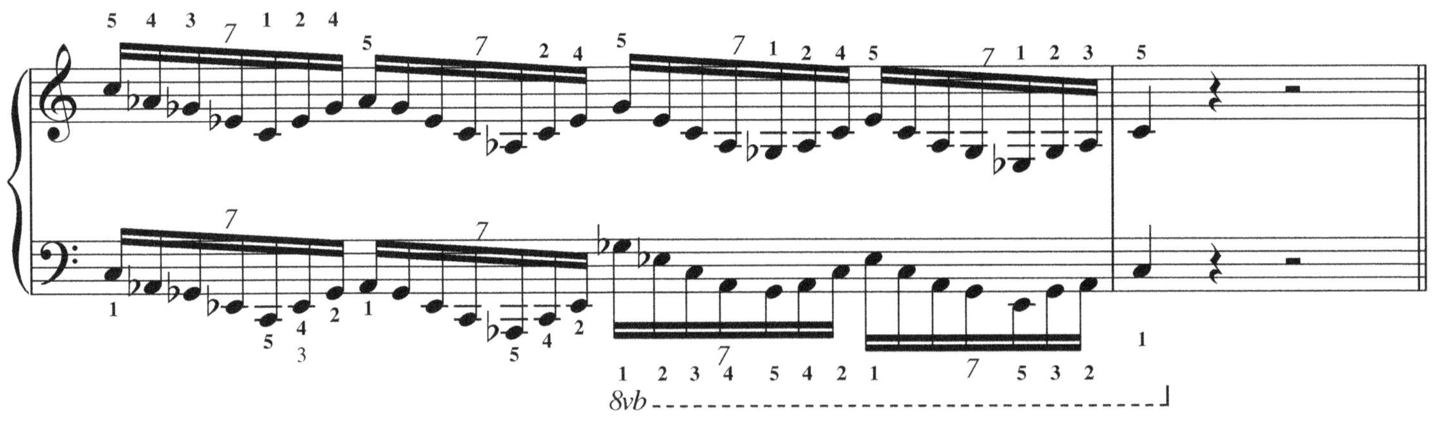

Apply the same patterns in the following chords:

Christos Tsitsaros

Christos Tsitsaros, contributing composer and arranger for the Hal Leonard Student Piano Library, is Professor of Piano Pedagogy at the University of Illinois. Born in Nicosia, Cyprus, he received his first formal instruction at the Greek Academy of Music. At the age of thirteen, he won first prize at the National Competition of the Conservatory of Athens. He later continued his musical studies at the Chopin Academy of Warsaw and later in Paris, receiving the Diplôme Supérieur d'Exécution with distinction. In 1986, a scholarship from the A. G. Leventis Foundation enabled him to pursue further development at the School of Music of Indiana University, where he received an Artist Diploma and a Masters degree (1989). He attained a Doctor of Musical Arts in Piano Performance from the University of Illinois (1993). His mentors include pianists Jan Ekier, Aldo Ciccolini, Jean-Claude Pennetier, Germaine Mounier, György Sebök, and Ian Hobson.

Dr. Tsitsaros has participated in various workshops and conferences as a performer and lecturer, and has appeared as soloist and recitalist in Europe, the United States, and Canada. In 2001, he gave his New York debut recital at Weill Carnegie Hall. Two CD recordings of his original piano compositions are available on the Centaur label. He currently serves as Piano Chair for the Illinois State Music Teachers Association.